Seattle Audubon Society

T0367038

REPTILES OF WASHINGTON AND OREGON

Coordinating Editors
Robert M. Storm
William P. Leonard

Written by
Herbert A. Brown
R. Bruce Bury
David M. Darda
Lowell V. Diller
Charles R. Peterson
Robert M. Storm

Seattle Audubon Society
Seattle, Washington

September 1995

Reptiles of Washington and Oregon
Copyright © 1995

ISBN 0-914516-12-4: $18.95

Published by Seattle Audubon Society, Seattle, Washington
Graphic design and production by Mary-Ellen Voss
Cover design and production by Lorie Ransom
Illustrations by Nikki McClure
Range maps produced by Kelly McAllister
Printed in Hong Kong by Mantec Production Company

To obtain additional copies of this book, call or write:
Seattle Audubon Society   (206)523-4483
8050 35th Avenue NE
Seattle, Washington 98115
www.seattleaudubon.org

Second Printing: July 2000
Third Printing: January 2006

Dedicated to the memory of Murray L. Johnson,
friend and colleague.

Murray L. Johnson

TABLE OF CONTENTS

Publisher's Preface vii

Introduction 1

Acknowledgments 3

Checklist of Washington and Oregon Reptiles 4

Overview of Reptiles (Robert M. Storm) 6

Notes on Turtles (R. Bruce Bury) 10

Notes on Lizards (Herbert A. Brown) 14

Notes on Snakes (Robert M. Storm) 19

Species Accounts:
Snapping Turtle (R. Bruce Bury) 28
Painted Turtle (R. Bruce Bury) 30
Western Pond Turtle (R. Bruce Bury) 34
Slider (R. Bruce Bury) 38
Loggerhead (R. Bruce Bury) 40
Green Turtle (R. Bruce Bury) 42
Pacific Ridley (R. Bruce Bury) 44
Leatherback (R. Bruce Bury) 46
Northern Alligator Lizard (Herbert A. Brown) 48
Southern Alligator Lizard (Robert M. Storm) 52
Mojave Black-collared Lizard (Robert M. Storm) 56
Long-nosed Leopard Lizard (Robert M. Storm) 60
Short-horned Lizard (Robert M. Storm) 64
Desert Horned Lizard (Robert M. Storm) 68
Sagebrush Lizard (Robert M. Storm) 72
Western Fence Lizard (Herbert A. Brown) 76
Side-blotched Lizard (Robert M. Storm) 80
Western Skink (Herbert A. Brown) 84
Western Whiptail (Robert M. Storm) 88
Plateau Striped Whiptail (Robert M. Storm) 92

Rubber Boa (Charles R. Peterson) 94
Racer (David M. Darda) 98
Sharptail Snake (David M. Darda) 102
Ring-necked Snake (David M. Darda) 106
Night Snake (Lowell V. Diller) 110
Common Kingsnake (David M. Darda) 114
California Mountain Kingsnake (David M. Darda) 118
Striped Whipsnake (Lowell V. Diller) 122
Gopher Snake (Lowell V. Diller) 126
Western Ground Snake (Lowell V. Diller) 130
Pacific Coast Aquatic Garter Snake (Charles R. Peterson) 134
Western Terrestrial Garter Snake (Charles R. Peterson) 138
Northwestern Garter Snake (Charles R. Peterson) 144
Common Garter Snake (Charles R. Peterson) 148
Western Rattlesnake (Lowell V. Diller) 154

Table 1 (Charles R. Peterson) 160

Figures (Nikki McClure) 161

General References 164

Selected Bibliography 165

Glossary of Selected Terms 168

Map of Washington and Oregon Counties 174

Note: Identified above within parenthesis is the name of the specific author of each chapter and species account.

PUBLISHER'S PREFACE

The mission of the Seattle Audubon Society is to assist its members to appreciate and preserve the birds, plants and animals occurring in the Pacific Northwest and the natural environments in which they are found. Important features of this book are clearly laid-out text, keys, maps, drawings and high-quality color photographs. This book is intended to be suitable for use by schools, colleges, the general public and wildlife biologists alike.

The publication of this book has been carried out entirely from funds provided by the Seattle Audubon Society. However, the Society and its members owe a particular debt of gratitude to the authors of this book, for not only did they agree to donate the manuscript to the Society, but they waived all royalties. Also, the photographers donated onetime use of their excellent photos. On behalf of all our members, I should like to offer our sincerest thanks to all who participated in the compilation of the manuscript. In particular, I would like to offer my own warmest thanks to Bill Leonard and Mary-Ellen Voss for being both competent and a pleasure to work with.

David Hutchinson
Publications Chair
Seattle Audubon Society
A Washington Non-profit Corporation

Other books available from Seattle Audubon Society:

Amphibians of the Pacific Northwest

Butterflies of Cascadia

Dragonflies of Washington

Field Guide to the Common Wetland Plants of Western Washington and Northwest Oregon

INTRODUCTION

This book is intended to help teachers, students, naturalists, professional field biologists and lay-persons to identify the reptiles of Washington and Oregon. The information herein is based on field studies and experiences by the authors and on published information. References used in the preparation of this book are listed in the references and bibliography sections. Readers are encouraged to look into these publications for more information on Washington and Oregon reptiles and on reptiles in general.

Using This Book

It is usually not necessary to capture reptiles to identify them. If captured, they should be handled as carefully and as briefly as possible and then returned to the capture site. When looking for reptiles in the field, avoid disrupting the habitat as much as possible, and try to replace rocks, logs, etc. to their original position.

After carefully examining the reptile from as close a distance as possible, look through the photographs in this guide for the closest match in appearance. Read the description of that species, paying special attention to the characteristics set in bold type. In addition, check the distribution map to make sure that the species should occur where it was found. If the description doesn't match the animal or the species name you decide on or doesn't occur in the area shown on the map, refer to the Similar Species section. Eventually, through a process of elimination, the reader should be able to correctly identify the animal. If a reptile is surely identified and found outside its indicated (normal) range, it should be carefully documented as to location of sighting, good photographs taken if possible, then reported to the nongame program of the state wildlife agency.

Organization of This Book

This book includes species accounts for the 35 species of reptiles that occur in Washington and Oregon and in the Pacific Ocean offshore from these states. The species accounts are first organized into families and then alphabetically by scientific name within families. Information on each species is presented under several headings that are discussed below.

Nomenclature: We have tried to use the most recent and widely accepted common and scientific names. It should be noted, however, that continued research by experts often leads to taxonomic revisions or name changes. We have relied upon Collins, J.T. 1990, *Standard common and scientific names for North American amphibians and reptiles, S.S.A.R.: Herpetological Circular No. 19*, except for the Garter Snakes where we recognize Rossman, D.A., N.B. Ford and R.A. Seigel, in press, *The garter snakes: evolution and ecology*. Scientific names are followed by the name(s) of the person(s) who described the species.

Names in parentheses indicate that the genus has been changed since being described.

Description: The species descriptions present characteristics that are most useful for properly identifying a turtle, lizard or snake. The descriptions apply to mature animals, but juveniles are also described if they differ appreciably from adults. The key characteristics, or field marks, are highlighted in bold type. Lengths are given in both inches and millimeters. Lengths of lizards are given as the maximal known snout-vent length, with tail length (if mentioned) given as a proportion of snout-vent length (e.g., tail length about twice the snout-vent length). Snake lengths are given as maximal total lengths, and for turtles maximal upper shell (carapace) lengths are given.

Similar Species: This section provides the names and a brief description of the other reptiles that have a similar appearance. The accounts of the species in this section should be studied closely when making difficult identifications.

Distribution: This section focuses on a species' geographical and elevational distribution in Washington and Oregon. However, in many cases the maximum elevation a species occurs at is not precisely known. The accompanying range maps show the areas where each species is known to have been found in our area.

Habits and Habitat: This section briefly covers the life history of the species and describes the places in which it lives. Information is included on the animal's diet, predators, behavior and breeding biology.

Remarks: Here we have placed information that we thought would be of interest to our readers but that did not fit well under any of the other headings. The type of information in this section varies but often deals with taxonomy and status.

ACKNOWLEDGMENTS

Many individuals made a significant contribution to the preparation of this book. Mike Adams, John Applegarth, Jon Beck, Ed Bowlby, Scott Eckert, James Harding, Peter Pritchard, William Radke, and Kate Slavens loaned us many 35 mm color slides, some of which are reproduced in this book. We are most grateful to the following individuals for reviewing and providing valuable comments on portions of this manuscript: Paul Bartelt; Edmund Brodie III; Sean Doody; Mike Dorcas; Scott Eckert; and Amy Lind. Richard Seigel kindly provided information that was in press. The authors also wish to acknowledge the following individuals whose field work and publications on Pacific Northwest reptiles have benefited this manuscript: Edwin Bell; Jon Beck; Jeff Boundy; Edmund Brodie, Jr.; Edmund Brodie III; David Clayton; Charlie Crisafulli; Steven Cross; Mike Dorcas; Henry Fitch; David Good; Steven Herman; Don Johnson; Murray L. Johnson; Warren Jones; Colin Leingang; Amy Lind; Steve Manlow; Kelly McAllister; Richard Nauman; Ronald Nussbaum; Jim Riggs; Douglas Rossman; James Slater; Robert C. Stebbins; Alan D. St. John; Todd Thompson; Ernie Wagner; and Richard Wallace. We are also deeply indebted to Seattle Audubon's publications chair, David Hutchinson, for his constant support for this project.

The range maps were prepared by Kelly R. McAllister with input from the authors, John Applegarth, Alan D. St. John, and Jim Riggs. Kelly also provided us with many of the elevation records for Washington. We would also like to express our gratitude to the following institutions for providing information from their herpetological collections for use in creating the distribution maps: American Museum of Natural History; Auburn University; Brigham Young University; California Academy of Sciences; University of California, Berkeley; University of Colorado; Florida Museum of Natural History; Field Museum of Natural History, Chicago; Fort Worth Museum of Science and Industry; Harvard Museum of Comparative Zoology; University of Idaho; Illinois Natural History Survey; University of Illinois at Champaign-Urbana; Southern Illinois University; University of Kansas; Los Angeles County Museum; Louisiana State University; Michigan State University; University of Michigan; University of Missouri, Columbia; United States National Museum; New Mexico State University; North Carolina Museum of Natural History; University of Oklahoma; Oregon State University; Pacific Lutheran University; University of Puget Sound; Strecker Museum at Baylor University; Texas A&M University; Tulane University; University of Texas at El Paso; Walla Walla College; Washington State University; University of Washington; and Yale University.

The authors and editors also thank their families for their love and support through the completion of this project.

Bob Storm,	Bill Leonard,	Herb Brown,	
Bruce Bury,	Dave Darda,	Lowell Diller,	Chuck Peterson

CHECKLIST OF WASHINGTON AND OREGON REPTILES

CLASS	**Reptilia:**	Reptiles

ORDER	**Testudines:**	Turtles

FAMILY	**Chelydridae:**	Snapping Turtles

❏ Snapping Turtle *(Chelydra serpentina)*   {I}

FAMILY	**Emydidae:**	Emydid Turtles

❏ Painted Turtle *(Chrysemys picta)*
❏ Western Pond Turtle *(Clemmys marmorata)*
❏ Common Slider *(Trachemys scripta)*   {I}

FAMILY	**Cheloniidae:**	Sea Turtles

❏ Loggerhead *(Caretta caretta)*
❏ Green Turtle *(Chelonia mydas)*
❏ Pacific Ridley *(Lepidochelys olivacea)*

FAMILY	**Dermochelyidae:**	Leatherback Sea Turtles

❏ Leatherback *(Dermochelys coriacea)*

ORDER	**Squamata:**	Lizards, Amphisbaenians, and Snakes

SUBORDER	**Sauria:**	Lizards

FAMILY	**Anguidae:**	Anguids

❏ Northern Alligator Lizard *(Elgaria coerulea)*
❏ Southern Alligator Lizard *(Elgaria multicarinata)*

FAMILY	**Iguanidae:**	Iguanids

❏ Mojave Black-collared Lizard *(Crotaphytus bicinctores)*
❏ Long-nosed Leopard Lizard *(Gambelia wislizenii)*
❏ Short-horned Lizard *(Phrynosoma douglassii)*
❏ Desert Horned Lizard *(Phrynosoma platyrhinos)*
❏ Sagebrush Lizard *(Sceloporus graciosus)*
❏ Western Fence Lizard *(Sceloporus occidentalis)*
❏ Side-blotched Lizard *(Uta stansburiana)*

FAMILY	**Scincidae:**	Skinks

❏ Western Skink *(Eumeces skiltonianus)*

FAMILY	**Teiidae**	Whiptails, Racerunners, and Ground Lizards

❏ Western Whiptail *(Cnemidophorus tigris)*
❏ Plateau Striped Whiptail *(Cnemidophorus velox)* {I}

SUBORDER	**Serpentes:**	Snakes

FAMILY	**Boidae:**	Boas and Pythons

❏ Rubber Boa *(Charina bottae)*

FAMILY	**Colubridae:**	Colubrids

❏ Racer *(Coluber constrictor)*
❏ Sharptail Snake *(Contia tenuis)*
❏ Ringneck Snake *(Diadophis punctatus)*
❏ Night Snake *(Hypsiglena torquata)*
❏ Common Kingsnake *(Lampropeltis getula)*
❏ California Mountain Kingsnake *(Lampropeltis zonata)*
❏ Striped Whipsnake *(Masticophis taeniatus)*
❏ Gopher Snake *(Pituophis catenifer)*
❏ Western Ground Snake *(Sonora semiannulata)*
❏ Pacific Coast Aquatic Garter Snake *(Thamnophis atratus)*
❏ Western Terrestrial Garter Snake *(Thamnophis elegans)*
❏ Northwestern Garter Snake *(Thamnophis ordinoides)*
❏ Common Garter Snake *(Thamnophis sirtalis)*

FAMILY	**Viperidae:**	Pit Vipers and Vipers

❏ Western Rattlesnake *(Crotalus viridis)*

{I} = species introduced to Washington and Oregon

OVERVIEW OF REPTILES

R eptiles evolved from anthracosaurian amphibians at least 300,000,000 years
ago in the late Paleozoic. Among these earliest-known forms were
synapsid reptiles (one lateral opening in the temporal area on each side of the
skull), which diverged from the main reptile line to become the earliest mammals by the end of the Paleozoic. Late in the Paleozoic, early reptiles again
branched, with one arm being the Anapsida (no temporal openings in skull)
from which evolved the turtles early in the Mesozoic. The second arm or line,
the Diapsida (two temporal openings on each side), are now considered to have
developed in two major directions during the late Paleozoic or early Mesozoic;
namely, the archosaurs and the lepidosaurs.

Archosaurs further diverged into a line from which came all the dinosaurs,
the pterosaurs (flying reptiles) and the birds, and a line that led to the crocodilians (probably in the early Mesozoic). Lepidosaur fossils first appear in late
Paleozoic deposits and represent early *Sphenodon* (Tuatara) ancestral types
during the early Mesozoic. These early sphenodontids disappeared as fossils
during the late Mesozoic, and there are no Cenozoic fossils between those forms
and the single present-day species, the Tuatara. Squamate reptiles (lizards and
snakes) also evolved in the lepidosaur line, lizards first appearing in the fossil
record in the late Jurassic part of the Mesozoic. Some of these earliest lizards
can be related to modern lizard categories. Snakes first show up in mid-
Cretaceous deposits, but the earliest snakes were not related to living snake
families and left no descendant forms in later fossil records.

It is quite apparent from the above that turtles represent a very ancient
lineage, long separated from other reptile lines. Today, as the order Testudines,
they are a world-wide group of some 230 species. Although not as ancient as
turtles, crocodilians also diverged from other reptiles early in the Mesozoic and
are considered by some to be more related to birds than to modern reptiles. They
survive in the warmer areas of the earth as the order Crocodylia, consisting of
crocodiles, alligators, caimans and gavials; there are some 23 species in the
order. The order Sphenodontida is represented by one living species, the
Tuatara *(Sphenodon punctatus)*, which occurs on islands near New Zealand.
The lizards and snakes (order Squamata), although appearing relatively late in
the fossil record, have been by far the most successful in terms of numbers and
radiation into numerous niches. There are over 5000 squamate reptile species in
existence today, including lizards (3,300 species), snakes (2,700 species) and
worm lizards (140 species). Lizards and snakes are widespread in the temperate
and tropical areas of the world, while worm lizards are limited to the tropics and
subtropics. Only turtles, lizards and snakes occur in the Pacific Northwest.

Two notable early developments in the amphibian-reptile transition
contributed more than anything else to the early success of reptiles. The first of
these was a modification of the bones and muscles of the jaw that enabled much

greater pressure to be exerted on food items, allowing the owner to seize and crush insects. The second was the development of the shelled amniote egg, which freed vertebrates from a dependence on water for reproduction. The amniote egg contains a sack of water (the amnion) which is considerably protected from evaporation by a leathery or calcareous shell. The egg also contains abundant yolk and must be fertilized before the shell is formed, thus requiring internal fertilization.

As a group, reptiles have a dry scaly skin with fewer skin glands than amphibians. They breath largely by means of lungs, but several aquatic forms (e.g., some turtles and snakes) as well as some terrestrial species can carry on gas exchange through the skin. This may amount to almost a third of total respiration in some. Respiration through mouth and throat tissues is known to occur during lengthy immersions or hibernation in some turtles. Turtles and squamate reptiles are usually said to have three-chambered hearts, but the detailed structure of such hearts are now known to vary considerably according to the way of life of the owner. The single ventricle is often partially divided into three sub-chambers, resulting in a primitive "five-chambered" heart. In crocodilians the ventricle is completely divided giving those animals a four-chambered heart. As mentioned above, fertilization is internal in reptiles. Sperm are usually transferred into the female's cloaca by a penis, which is everted through the cloacal opening from the floor of the cloaca in turtles and crocodilians and from the base of the tail in lizards and snakes. The penis is a double structure in lizards and snakes and the pair are known as hemipenes (singular hemipenis). The shelled amniote egg is susceptible to drying and must be placed in somewhat moist surroundings or retained in the female's body for development.

Reptiles are often referred to as cold-blooded, implying that they always have much cooler body temperatures than birds and mammals. They are more properly called ectothermic which means that their body temperatures are largely determined by sources of heat outside of their body (versus birds and mammals, which are endothermic). Reptiles, especially lizards and snakes, have evolved ectothermy to a high degree, such that during their periods of activity they may maintain body temperatures comparable to or even higher than those of endotherms. This is done largely by behavioral means of which the following are some examples: The reptile can control the amount of time spent in the sun (basking), moving in and out of the sunlight, it can control orientation to the sun (facing the sun, back to the sun, etc.) and it can control the amount of the body that is in the sun (especially snakes). Reptiles that warm mainly by sunlight are called heliotherms (most lizards); those that derive heat from warm surfaces are called thigmotherms. Hundreds of thigmothermic snakes are killed each year as they absorb heat from paved roads. It should be added that most reptiles probably utilize both methods of warming at various times in their life.

Some non-behavioral mechanisms may also be used by some reptiles to contribute to temperature regulation. One that can be seen in some lizards (e.g.,

Western Fence Lizard and Long-nosed Leopard Lizard) and some snakes (certain rattlesnakes) is a lightening and darkening of the skin by means of regulating the pigment distribution within certain deep skin cells. Cool lizards are darker and thus absorb more heat; as they warm up, the skin lightens and reflects heat more efficiently. There are also mechanisms that increase blood flow to the skin during basking or control blood flow to the head, allowing differential warming of the body and head.

Concerning temperature regulation, different reptile species vary greatly in terms of their active or preferred temperatures and in terms of the temperatures that they can be active at. There is some evidence that activity temperatures may show similarities within a given genus or even within a systematic family. Highest activity temperatures occur in lizards of hot deserts, such as the Desert Iguana of southern California and Arizona deserts, which is active at body temperatures of 40°-42° C (104°-107.6° F). At the lowest extreme, the Tuatara *(Sphenodon)*, which is largely nocturnal on islands off New Zealand, has been shown to be active at body temperatures of 6.2°-18° C (43°-64° F), a range more typical of a salamander. Between these two extremes are a variety of temperature regimes, the variations being related to such things as systematic group, environmental habitat and climate, way of life (i.e., nocturnal or diurnal, herbivore or carnivore, active hunter or sit-and-wait predator, etc.), and probably to such things as age, sex and reproductive status.

Our desert lizards such as the Long-nosed Leopard Lizard and the Western Whiptail are most active at body temperatures of 37°-40° C (98.6°-104° F), while the Sagebrush Lizard prefers temperatures of 30°-38° C (86°-100.4° F), with a mean around 34° C (93.2° F). Southern Alligator Lizards inhabit fairly dry brushy areas in our region (both east and west of the Cascades) and field measurements on this species in southern California showed that it is active over a wide range of body temperatures, 9.4°-33.8° C (49°-93° F). Most of our snakes and lizards have not been accurately measured with respect to temperature, but we can expect higher temperatures in desert forms and lower ones in forms inhabiting the western parts of our states. In general, snakes in a given area average lower body temperatures than do lizards.

Because they are ectothermic, reptiles are largely unable to cope physiologically with problems of overheating or overcooling. In this respect, it is notable that activity temperatures of many reptiles are often within only a few degrees of what is called an upper lethal, a body temperature that would incapacitate or kill the animal if it got that high. Most reptiles avoid this by being inactive in cooler retreats during high temperature periods. Active Long-nosed Leopard Lizards have been seen to stand with all their toes arched away from the hot soil, to wriggle their body and tail to expose cooler subsurface soil and to climb into desert shrubs to avoid higher ground surface temperatures. Many lizards pant during hot weather in order to cause cooling evaporation from mouth and throat surfaces. Overcooling is an even greater danger to reptiles, because below a certain body temperature they are helpless to move to warmer areas. There is considerable evidence that winter mortality among hibernating reptiles is often severe.

It is evident that ectothermy has not been a great handicap to reptiles. They have evolved behaviors and physiologies that have enabled them to exist quite successfully along with endotherms. Reptiles have been called low energy machines because their energy requirements are much less than those of comparable-sized endotherms (birds and mammals); i.e., a tenth or a fifth as much, or even lower. Reptiles are capable of fairly brief spurts of high energy activity, but are incapable of sustained high expenditures of energy. In other words, most of their life is slow-moving, but they can chase a prey animal briefly or escape from predators with short dashes, but can't sustain long chases or long active escapes from danger. Their fluctuating temperatures are closely related to this low energy consumption and the evolutionary fine-tuning of this combination has enabled reptiles, particularly the squamate types, to spread over much of the world and succeed in many habitats.

NOTES ON TURTLES

Turtles Species Diversity and Distribution

Turtles occur on all the major temperate and tropical land masses, being absent only from the colder parts of these lands. They also occur widely as marine forms in all the warmer seas. There are about 257 species of turtles worldwide, divided into 11 families, including 91 species of emydid turtles (the family of aquatic and semiaquatic turtles that includes most North American species), 109 other freshwater turtles, 50 tortoises and seven sea turtles. We have 48 species in seven families in North America north of Mexico as follows: three species of snapping turtles, eight musk and mud turtles, 25 emydids (semiaquatic and pond turtles), three tortoises, three softshell turtles, five marine turtles and one leatherback (another sea turtle).

Although a relatively small group of vertebrates, turtles have a remarkably long lineage. Turtles had developed their characteristic shell over 200 million years ago and evolved through the Age of Dinosaurs to the present. Turtles usually are grouped with crocodilians and snake-lizards in the Class Reptilia, but turtles and crocodilians are distinct lineages; crocodilians are now thought to be more closely related to birds than other reptiles, whereas turtles evolved so early that their affinities are either unclear or represent a very ancient separation from other reptiles.

Despite the fact that Oregon and Washington are biologically diverse, the turtle fauna here is depauperate and apparently has been for a long time (i.e., few fossil species). There are two native freshwater turtles (emydids) regionally, the Western Pond Turtle and the Painted Turtle. The Western Pond Turtle has a fossil history back at least to the Pliocene (e.g., fossils occur in Nevada) and today lives only along the West Coast from Washington to northern Baja California. Painted Turtles appear to have arrived in Oregon and Washington in more recent times, perhaps spreading west through the Columbia River Gorge. The Painted Turtle has one of the largest ranges for a North American species, occurring from the Pacific Northwest to the Atlantic Coast and from Louisiana to southern Canada.

Some Characteristics of Turtles

All turtles have a primitive vertebrate skull pattern (anapsid skull), in which the sides of the skull behind the eye cavities are solid, whereas all other reptiles, as well as birds and mammals, have one or two openings per side in this (temporal) area. Turtles lack true teeth, but most possess some version of sharp-edged horny ridges on the jaw margins that serve as teeth. The limb girdles (pectoral and pelvic) of turtles have somehow evolved to a location inside the rib cage, unlike the situation in all other vertebrates where they are external to the rib cage.

Most turtles have a distinctive shape and shell, familiar to everyone. The carapace (upper shell) has about 50 underlying bones and the plastron (lower shell) has 11 bones, and the two shells are usually joined by a strong bridge. The bony foundation is overlaid with scutes (composed of horn or keratin, as are scales). For example, the carapace of the Western Pond Turtle has 37 scutes: five vertebral (down the center of the back), four costals on each side (broad scutes) and 12 marginals on each side (edging the shell). The seams of the scutes usually do not overlap those of the bones, which adds strength. These bones and scutes form a strong box-like structure in most species, and most turtles can withdraw the head and appendages into the shell for protection from predators. Some species have a reduced plastron (e.g., Snapping Turtles), lack a hard covering (e.g., Softshell Turtles) or have plastron hinges (e.g., Box Turtles).

Courtship and Reproduction

Courtship and mating occur in the water in freshwater and marine turtles, but on land among tortoises and box turtles. A Red-eared Slider (*Trachemys*) or a Painted Turtle (*Chrysemys*) male positions himself in front of and facing the female and maintains this position, even if it means swimming backward. From time to time, the male extends his forelegs toward the female and vibrates his elongated claws against the sides of her head. After the female eventually responds to this stimulation, the pair sinks to the bottom and copulates. Marine turtles court and copulate offshore immediately after the female has laid her eggs on the adjacent beach.

Sex and species recognition are probably largely visual in aquatic turtles, but are more likely by both vision and olfaction (smell) in land forms. In the Gopher Tortoises of the southeastern United States, the male bobs his head rapidly as he approaches the female, possibly to help spread his scent toward her. After reaching her, he repeatedly bites her on the head, legs and shell. This continues as they circle one another, eventually ending in copulation. Giant Tortoises (*Testudo*) are said to pound on the female's shell as part of their courtship.

Male turtles possess a single grooved penis, located on the floor of the cloaca, which can be everted through the cloacal opening for intromission into the cloaca of the female. Copulation in turtles may involve what seems to us somewhat awkward positions by the male, but insemination is usually success-ful. Among some turtles, viable sperm can be stored in the female's reproduc-tive system for up to four years.

All turtles are oviparous (egg-laying) and the eggs are always buried by the female in the ground or in decaying plant material. All female turtles are able to dig deep flask-shaped egg holes with their rear feet, whether these be the flexible feet of a Pond or Painted Turtle, the flipper-like feet of a marine turtle or the stump-like feet of a Desert Tortoise. The eggs are spherical or ovoid, white in color, and have a shell that varies from leathery to calcareous. Number of eggs in a clutch varies from a dozen or so in most freshwater turtles (however, up to 80 in Snapping Turtles) to 200-300 in marine turtles. Further reproductive details are given in the individual species accounts. It has been learned recently that the incubation temperature of the eggs determines the sex of the hatchlings in many (but not all) species of turtles. In one study, Painted Turtle nests subjected to relatively high temperatures (mean July air temperatures were 23° C or greater) produced over half female hatchlings; at 25° C, all hatchlings were females. Nests with lower temperatures produced males. Therefore, nests placed in an open southern exposure would result in more female offspring. Male hatchlings would result from sites with less solar insulation (e.g., northern aspect) or shaded nests (including sites that become overgrown with vegetation). Further, general summer temperatures are a major influence on sex determination of hatchlings, so that more females would hatch out after a warmer than normal summer and vice versa for cooler summers.

Age, Size and Growth

The growth of young turtles is rapid in their early years, slowing down considerably as they get older. In large turtles such as sea turtles and tortoises, early growth rates can be quite impressive. A captive hatchling Loggerhead Turtle attained a weight of 80 pounds (36 kg) in four and one-half years. Captive tortoises (*Testudo*) from the Galapagos Islands have almost tripled their weight in two years.

Sexual maturity in turtles seems to be more a matter of size than of age. For example, Slider (*Trachemys*) males become sexually mature at a plastron length of 3.5 to 3.9 inches (9 to 10 cm) when they are anywhere from two to five years in age. Female Sliders mature at 5.9 to 7.7 inches (15 to 19.5 cm) in plastral length at ages of three to eight years. Surprisingly, some large species of turtles (e.g., Hawksbill) attain sexual maturity in about the same time as the smaller species (three to five years).

Turtles have a well-deserved reputation for longevity; many of our freshwater species live 40 or 50 years or longer. Giant tortoises perhaps hold the age record with one verified record of 152 years. There is apparently good evidence for Box Turtles (*Terrapene*) being able to live 80 to 120 years.

Remarks

Besides the two species of introduced turtles included in the species accounts, at least nine other introduced species now occur in Pacific Northwest waters, including the Reeve's Turtle (*Chinemys reevesi*) and Malayan Box Turtle (*Cuora amboinensis*), two Asian species that are commonly sold in pet stores. Of particular concern are introduced aquatic species that are increasingly found in the wild. These turtles are seldom detected because they rarely bask, and thus could become well-established before we realize it. Four turtle species from eastern North America are occasionally found in our area: Mud (*Kinosternon subrubrum*), Musk (*Sternotherus odoratus*), Softshell (*Apalone spiniferus*) and Box (*Terrapene sp.*). Although few Softshell Turtles have been found, one record near Portland, Oregon was of a nesting female. Softshell Turtles are pugnacious when handled and can inflict a deep bite.

Federal health regulations require that turtles shipped across state lines be over four inches long, which reduces the likelihood that bacteria poisoning will be passed from turtles to humans. The regulation was aimed at hatchling turtles, which carry *Salmonella* (a bacteria found in turtles, other wildlife and raw foods). The small turtles were once sold by the millions every year, and cases of *Salmonella* poisoning were tied to small turtles in homes. Other contributing factors to the health hazard were turtle tanks fouled by the turtles and their food (particularly hamburger), and poor hygiene (e.g., kids who handled turtles and then put their fingers in their mouths). Hatchling turtles from U.S. breeders are still sold in Canada, Asia and Europe.

Pet turtles are released into nature when people tire of them, don't want to treat them when they become sick or are bitten by their turtle (e.g., Sliders have sharp beaks). Continued release and success of exotic turtles may lead to breeding populations of even more species in the Pacific Northwest. The addition of exotic, often colorful turtles to our fauna may seem benign or even to be encouraged, but introduced species such as starlings, carp and zebra mussels have wreaked havoc on many ecosystems. Exotic turtles might prove to be similarly harmful.

These introduced species may compete with or displace our native turtles. For example, the Western Pond Turtle is severely depleted in the Puget Sound region where the Slider has become common. Although there is no cause-and-effect relationship established, the invasion of introduced turtles can be suspected as a cause of the decline of a native turtle. Turtles carry many parasites and diseases, some of which might be transmitted to native wildlife or humans (e.g., in the same manner as *Salmonella*). Further, pet turtles are released into the wild when they are sick (when they are at the most advanced stages of diseases). While this issue has not been well-addressed, serious concerns about the potential problems are warranted.

California has attempted to avert these problems by a ban on importation of noxious wildlife, including Snapping and Softshell Turtles. Also, a national effort to control exotic introductions is underway. However, we have little knowledge of the frequency or numbers of introduced turtles nor of studies of transmission of diseases or parasites between turtle species or from turtles to humans. An obvious remedy is that turtles from pet stores, or caught in the wild and kept for awhile and/or transported, should not be released. It is better to give them to a wildlife rehabilitation center, humane society or local wildlife department, where they will receive a new home and proper treatment. A responsible attitude is needed for the purchase of turtles, because they require specialized care and attention.

NOTES ON LIZARDS

Species Diversity and Distribution

Modern lizards and snakes are closely related, with lizards probably being a more generalized and primitive group. Snakes are specialized and derived from ancient lizards that lost their legs while developing subterranean burrowing habits and an elongate body form. Today, examples of an intermediate stage in this evolutionary transformation can be found in legless lizards and snakes with vestiges of hind legs. The total number of lizard species (3,300) exceeds that of snakes (2,700), and both groups are most successful in the sunnier and warmer climates of tropical and desert regions.

Washington and Oregon have diverse life zones, from deserts and grasslands to mountains and coniferous forests, but only twelve species of lizards inhabit this region. The colder temperatures of the Cascade Mountains and the cool cloudy weather of the western parts of these states have been significant barriers to the historical dispersal of lizards into these areas. The eastern portions of Washington and Oregon are hot and dry in the summer, but the winter season in this sagebrush/grassland is very cold and demands special survival adaptations. Only four lizard species occur fairly widely west of the Cascade Mountains; the Western Fence Lizard and the Southern Alligator Lizard inhabit relatively open and drier, often disturbed communities, while Northern Alligator Lizards and Western Skinks may penetrate forested habitats to some extent, or may occur in disturbed sites like roadsides or clearcuts. Eight other lizard species occur only in the dry open habitats of the interior.

This small fauna of lizards is represented by several distinct families. The family Iguanidae is the most diverse and includes the Mojave Black-collared Lizard, Long-nosed Leopard Lizard, Western Fence Lizard, Sagebrush Lizard, Side-blotched lizard, Desert Horned Lizard and Short-horned Lizard. The Western Skink belongs to the family Scincidae, the Plateau Striped and Western Whiptails are members of the family Teiidae, and the Southern and Northern Alligator Lizards are found in the family Anguidae.

Some Characteristics of Lizards

Snakes are easily recognized by their special body design, but lizards are sometimes confused with salamanders, because both have a similar body plan of head, trunk, tail and four legs. However, lizards have better adaptations for living on land than salamanders, as follows: 1) There are flexible but protective scales covering the body. 2) Sharp claws on fingers and toes facilitate climbing upon steep rock surfaces and the bark of trees. 3) Alert lizards rapidly respond to changes in their environment by using sensitive hearing ability that covers a wide range of sound frequencies and eyes with the capacity of distant vision and color perception. 4) Lizards have a complex brain that controls elaborate patterns of instinctive behavior and permits limited ability to learn from experience. 5) The lizard respiratory system includes paired lungs that increase absorption of oxygen into the blood, permitting higher metabolism, greater muscular effort and rapid locomotory activity. 6) Most lizards have a large nutrient-rich egg, covered by internal membranes and a protective shell that allow embryos to develop in their own freshwater "pond" (amniotic fluid) while the egg is buried on land in a hidden and sometimes protected (by a parent) nest.

Seasonal Patterns of Activity and Body Temperature

During the winter, all lizards in the Pacific Northwest hibernate from about October to February or March. The spring season is dominated by territorial displays and courtship, and the summer is a season for growth of juveniles and adults. Hatchlings appear in late summer and then grow slowly as they continue feeding for a few weeks after the adults have retreated to hibernation sites.

Most lizards are diurnal in their activity, and all lizards are ectotherms and poikilotherms (i.e., they have a variable body temperature that is dependent upon external environmental sources of heat). Active coordinated movements and normal behavior begin after an optimal body temperature for that particular species is achieved. Most lizards reach their preferred or optimal temperature by perching on some exposed surface where they can bask in the heat of the sun. They may also derive body heat by conduction from warm surfaces beneath their body. Lizards are often inactive during the hottest time of the day, especially in mid- to late summer, usually using cooler sub-surface retreats to avoid overheating. In contrast to lizards, birds and mammals (called endotherms or homeotherms) have relatively constant high body temperatures (about 39° or 40° C), produced by internal chemical and physiological mechanisms.

During the autumn season, lizards are daily exposed to shorter day lengths and longer, colder nights, and this environmental change acts to depress activity and promote return to a known hibernation site. Fall can be a stressful time for hatchlings hibernating for the first time, and this age group often suffers high mortality during the winter.

Courtship and Reproduction

Upon emergence from hibernation, adult lizards show low levels of activity for a few weeks, and much time is devoted to basking at protected sites close to an escape route. Males generally emerge from hibernation first, and females a few weeks later. Reproduction in Northwest lizards is strongly seasonal, with mating taking place in the spring and young appearing in late summer or early fall. The increasing day lengths and warmer temperatures of March and April stimulate the release of certain hormones, which promote maturation of reproductive organs (ovaries and testes), initiating territorial behavior and courtship. Adult males of some species, basking at some spot in their home range, will rapidly respond to the presence of an intruding male of the same species. They react by performing more or less elaborate stereotyped behavioral displays (e.g., rapid head-bobbing and push-ups, using the front legs). These actions frequently result in fights between males, and this aggressiveness helps to establish the boundaries of a dominant male's breeding territory.

Male lizards are often larger and more colorful than females, and these features improve a male's effectiveness in the defense of a territory. Large body size provides increased strength and leads to greater success in competitive encounters. Bright colors are a signal of sexual maturity and may serve to reduce fighting by warning off subordinate males. The distinctive color patterns and displays of male lizards also serve to attract and stimulate females to accept mating by the favored males. Courtship activities consume much time and energy, and male lizards frequently lose most of their fat reserves during the spring breeding season.

During mating, male lizards usually grasp the neck skin of the female with their jaws (male horned lizards grasp one of the female's horns). During this grasp, one of a pair of intromittent organs (hemipenes) is used to transfer sperm into the female's cloaca, where they can be stored in special tubules for many weeks.

During the spring months, eggs grow in the ovaries of the female, enlarging as they accumulate nutrients from fat stored in the abdomen or tail. The size and number of eggs produced by a female is partly dependent upon the amount of stored fat that accumulated during feeding activity of the previous summer! Fat bodies are not important for winter survival, but are necessary for successful reproduction in the spring.

Lizards in the Pacific Northwest show two modes of reproduction. Most species lay shell-covered eggs (oviparous) and shelter them under logs or rocks, or bury them in sand, soil or rotting vegetation, and then show no further care. The incubation period to hatching is generally eight to ten weeks and the hatchlings take care of themselves. In two species (Northern Alligator Lizard and Short-horned Lizard), the female retains the eggs until they are ready to hatch (viviparous) and the young are born alive. The egg has no shell covering and a placenta develops that allows the transfer of water and oxygen from the mother's blood to the embryo. The mother provides protection to the internally developing embryos and carries them to warm microhabitats where they may develop at a much faster rate than might occur in a cool, damp underground nest. This mode also reduces the chance of infections from soil bacteria or fungi that might kill the eggs or embryos.

Age, Size and Growth

Populations of a lizard species generally show some distinct age classes, based upon obvious size differences (e.g., juveniles, subadults, and adults). The life span of lizards is quite variable, but small-bodied species usually live for one or two years after reaching maturity, while large-bodied species may live for seven to nine years. The growth rates of lizards can be very irregular and

16

depends on many factors, such as amount of food and water, temperature, age, sex and breeding status. For many lizards the growth rate is greatest during the first year of life and slows down thereafter until some maximum size is reached. During the breeding season, sexually mature adults slow down or suppress body growth in favor of diverting energy to reproductive efforts. In some lizards the males have a relatively short life span and grow rapidly to reach sexual maturity, while females grow more slowly and have a longer life. There are many variations on this theme and each species, or population, may show different adaptations in their natural history.

Many species of lizards may show the growth of a new tail, and this regeneration process represents a type of survival tactic. The tail can be purposely discarded (autotomy) at a breakage point during attack by a predator (bird, snake or another lizard). The lizard, commonly seized by the tail, can escape while the predator's attention is directed at the vigorously moving tail, which may be brightly colored. Herpetologists use the frequency of tail regeneration as a guide to measure the intensity of predation pressure upon a lizard population. Sometimes the regeneration process is abnormal and double or triple new tails appear, and these unusual lizards may remind us (if we use our imagination) of ancient dinosaurs with spiked tails.

Food and Feeding

The feeding habits of lizards suggest that most species are indiscriminate carnivores (insectivores), and feed upon a wide variety of insects and spiders. Lizards have numerous small sharp teeth and relatively powerful jaw muscles, and are able to quickly seize and devour any commonly available food item of the right size. In terms of foraging strategy, some lizards are active searchers (Western Skink and Western Whiptail Lizard) and others (Western Fence Lizard and Mojave Black-collared Lizard) will rest for long periods at a sit-and-wait perch and then pursue moving prey items. The Long-nosed Leopard Lizard and some collared lizards are known to catch and eat other lizards, even members of the same species. Horned lizards feed largely on ants.

Enemies and Defense

Lizards have many enemies, but when they have reached their preferred body temperature, they are very alert and can present a real challenge to predaceous birds (Jays, Crows and Hawks), mammals (Foxes, Coyotes or even Chipmunks), and reptiles (Garter Snakes, Racers and Whipsnakes). Lizards may rely upon cryptic body coloration for concealment and/or upon rapid flight to escape such actives predators. Lizards may be especially vulnerable as they rest in hidden sites at night, allowing their temperatures to drop and becoming slow and awkward in movement. The sharp spiny scales of some lizards can help to hold the body tightly in narrow crevices, thus preventing removal, especially when the lungs inflate with air and expand the body diameter. When seized, alligator lizards violently twist the body and release foul-smelling fecal waste (solid and liquid) over the face of a predator. Mojave Black-collared Lizards and Western Fence Lizards intimidate would-be predators by biting with great ferocity. The bright blue tail of the Western Skink draws the predator's attention to this expendable section of the body, and following discarding of the tail, the vulnerable head/trunk region can escape into cover.

Biodiversity and Lizards

Every species of organism is a unique experiment in the process of adaptive evolution of life on earth, and each organism interacts with others at many different biotic levels in a small community or a large ecosystem. Every species of lizard also plays a role in sustaining a biological community. They are important members of the food web wherein lizards are consumed by a variety of bird and mammal predators; in turn, lizards are major predators of many kinds of insects, spiders and other small invertebrates. Lizards represent a specialized kind of vertebrate life, and they provide research biologists with simple model systems that may reveal answers to complex patterns and processes of vertebrate life, ranging from physiology, behavior and ecology to reproduction and development. Lizards are fascinating vertebrate animals, long admired by children and scientists alike, and they have made many important contributions to human welfare. They deserve our respect and admiration in our attempts to conserve natural environments and maintain the beauty and uniqueness of wildlife.

NOTES ON SNAKES

In evolutionary terms, snakes are the youngest major group of reptiles. They are in the order Squamata with lizards, but branched away from lizards, probably in the early Cretaceous (about 120 million years ago). The lizard group to which monitors belong (varanoids) is thought to have given rise to snakes early in varanoid history. Earliest snakes were probably burrowing types, but they have radiated widely away from these beginnings and most snake species today are surface dwellers, specialized for aquatic, terrestrial or arboreal ways of life. Snakes reach their greatest abundance and diversity in the warmer parts of the earth.

There are about 2,700 species of snakes in the world, forming the suborder Serpentes. They are usually divided into 12 systematic families, of which only three have members in the Northwest. Perhaps the most primitive snakes are small "blind" burrowing forms occurring largely in tropical areas. "Blind" is a misnomer because they possess tiny well-differentiated eyes, but they are usually covered by scales and appear as darkly pigmented spots. They are probably only sensitive to light intensities. The most advanced snakes are considered to be the highly poisonous types, the elapids (cobras, mambas, coral snakes, etc.) and the viperids (vipers, rattlesnakes, etc.). Perhaps the most specialized snakes are the poisonous sea snakes (family Hydrophidae, or sometimes classified as a subfamily of the elapids), which are entirely marine in warm oceans, never coming to land. The tail of sea snakes is flattened into an oar-like sculling organ.

Of the many species of snakes, only 15 kinds occur in Oregon and Washington, and several of these are at or near the northern limits of their distribution. As with lizards, the Cascade Mountains have been somewhat of a barrier to distribution across our two states, but in terms of numbers of species eastern and western Oregon have about the same (11), whereas in Washington, there are more species in eastern parts of the state. Some garter snakes (e.g., Northwestern Garter Snake and Common Garter Snake) occur at fairly high elevations in mountainous areas. Other species appear to have made use of the Columbia Gorge to move from western to eastern parts of our area. The Ringneck Snake is widespread in western Oregon, but also occurs in small areas just east of the Cascades in the two states. This may also be true of the Sharptail Snake. A broad zone of intergradation between our two subspecies of Gopher Snake occurs just east of the Cascades in Oregon and seems to indicate gene flow through the Gorge. Isolated populations of the Mountain Kingsnake in south-central Washington and north-central Oregon may be evidence of this phenomenon. Striped Whipsnakes may have used low passes in the southern Oregon Cascades at some time in the past to reach the Rogue Valley of western Oregon.

Most of our snakes belong to the family Colubridae; only the Rubber Boa

(Boidae) and the Western Rattlesnake (Viperidae) are not colubrids. On a world-wide basis, the family Colubridae includes some 1,400 species or somewhat over half of the living kinds of snakes. Among the colubrids are a few rear-fanged snakes (opisthoglyphs), two of which are known to have fatally bitten humans. Our Night Snake has enlarged rear teeth with which it can inject venom into its food victims (usually small lizards), but it is harmless to humans. Our relatively small Rubber Boa is in the same family with the worlds largest snakes, the Boa Constrictor, Reticulated Python and Anaconda. Contrary to certain local beliefs, there are no poisonous Coral Snakes in the Northwest.

Some Characteristics of Snakes

Snakes can be distinguished from most legless lizards by the following two characteristics: Lack of movable eyelids and lack of external ear openings. Instead of lids, the eyes of snakes are covered by transparent scales known as brilles. When the snake sheds its skin, the outer layer of the brilles is also shed as part of the skin. In addition to the above differences, snakes have no internal limb girdles nor limbs, but a few have vestigial pelvic girdles and rudimentary hind limbs. In our area, only the Rubber Boa shows this characteristic, having a small black spur on each side of the cloaca; these are larger in the male and are used to stroke the female during copulation. Other unique characteristics of snakes are left lung reduced in size or absent and lack of a sternum (breast bone), middle ear and urinary bladder. Many of the skull bones of snakes are loosely joined and can be spread apart during the feeding process. The two sides of the lower jaw are usually joined by a stretchy ligament, which allows the two sides to move somewhat independently of one another as the snake slowly swallows prey items.

The main weapons of snakes for defense and for catching prey animals for food are their teeth. Most harmless snakes have numerous small backward-curved uniform teeth on upper and lower jaws; some species have two additional longitudinal rows on the roof of the mouth. These many small teeth are used to hold the prey while the snake squeezes it to death by suffocation (constriction) with its body, or to pull the prey into the mouth and throat as the snake alter-nately "walks" its jaws along the victim's body. Venomous snakes can be divided into three groups, based on evolutionary specializations of their teeth from the basic pattern outlined above. Rear-fanged or opisthoglyph snakes have enlarged rear teeth in the upper jaws, equipped with grooves along which venom can flow as they chew on their victims. Most of these species are harmless to man but fatal to their usual prey. Snakes with elongated front fangs are either proteroglyphs or solenoglyphs. Proteroglyphs possess fixed fangs that have grooves or central openings along which venom can be injected into a bite in the manner of a hypodermic needle. Cobras, mambas and coral snakes are well-known members of this group, as are the marine sea snakes. Solenoglyphs have the longest fangs of all snakes, and this is possible because the hollow fangs can be folded back against the roof of the mouth when not in use. Members of the family Viperidae (rattlesnakes, water moccasins, vipers, etc.) are solenoglyphs.

A few snakes may have binocular vision (the ability to train both eyes on a given object), but most probably see a different visual field with each eye. Studies of visual acuity in snakes have shown that most lack a fovea (area of sharpest definition) and that focusing is less efficient than in lizards. Snakes probably have a vision much like we have near the edge of our retinal field, a high ability to detect movement. The ears of snakes lack eardrums and internal ear cavities, having instead the inner ear on each side connected to the jawbone by a single bone, the columella. This arrangement apparently enables them to hear certain low frequency air-borne sounds, as well as to detect ground vibrations.

Snakes are notorious for their protrusible forked tongues, and anyone who has watched them for any length of time, as they move about, will have noticed that they often flick the tongue in and out repeatedly. This activity is associated with the sense of smell in snakes. When the tongue flicks out of the mouth, the tips pick up tiny particles of chemical compounds from the air or substrate and carry them into the mouth. On the roof of the mouth are two paired pits each of which leads to small blind sacs, lined with sensory cells. These were originally called Jacobson's organs, but are now known as vomeronasal organs (VNO). Particles picked up by the snake's tongue are conveyed to pads on the floor of the mouth, which then press against the pits of the VNO, conveying the particles into the VNO and sending a sensory message to the snake's brain. The message is probably in the nature of a combined taste and smell sensation. When the tongue is flicked out, the two tips are spread apart and touch the substrate at different points, enabling each tip to pick up a slightly different message. It has been discovered recently that this sort of "stereo-testing" is necessary to enable the snake to follow a trail, such as that left by a prey animal or prospective mate.

Rattlesnakes and other pit vipers possess a rather deep pit on each side of the head between eye and nostril, which is capable of detecting heat, such as the body heat of warm-blooded prey animals. Pythons and some boas have pits along the edges of their jaws, which can also detect warmth. Such heat detectors obviously serve a necessary function for snakes that forage for food at night. Among the rear-fanged snakes in the family Colubridae, whatever venom they may have is produced in Duvernoy's gland, which drains onto the enlarged and grooved rear teeth on the upper jaw. Proteroglyphs and solenoglyphs (e.g., cobras and rattlesnakes) do not have a Duvernoy's gland, but possess modified salivary glands that produce their venom. These glands are surrounded by muscles, which contract to force the poison through the hollow fangs. Rattlesnakes, at least, have control of these muscles, because they sometimes bite without injecting venom (known as a "dry bite").

Snake venoms are often referred to as hemotoxic (also known as cytolytic) or neurotoxic. Hemotoxins attack and break down cells of the blood and other tissues of the body, whereas neurotoxins paralyze nervous tissues, especially those of the respiratory system and the heart. Venoms are usually mixtures of these components in varying proportions. Most rattlesnakes have largely hemotoxic venom, and their bites may result in considerable very painful tissue destruction. Cobras and their relatives produce a mainly neurotoxic venom, which is fast-acting and less painful, but is responsible for more human deaths. Among our colubrid supposedly non-venomous snakes, there is considerable evidence that the saliva of the Ringneck Snake is able to paralyze its small prey animals, being introduced into the victim as the snake chews along its body. It has been discovered that a few people may be highly allergic to what are usually harmless bites, such as those from a Garter Snake.

Patterns of Activity

All of our Northwestern snakes hibernate during the colder months of the year, utilizing a variety of shelters for protection. These hibernation sites must remain warm enough to prevent death by freezing, they must be of a suitable humidity, neither too dry nor too wet, and they must be adequately ventilated. During their winter "sleep", the snakes have greatly lowered metabolism, but they are still alive and must have certain minimum requirements to stay alive. Hibernation is a dangerous period and often results in winter fatalities. Hibernation sites may be underground in rodent burrows, within decaying logs or stumps, deep within old root systems of dead trees, or within crevices in rock outcrops or talus slopes, to mention some of the more important ones. More than one species may utilize the same hibernaculum. Four species of snakes were thought to be preparing to use an old fir stump for hibernation in western Oregon (Rubber Boa, Ringneck Snake, Racer and Gopher Snake). Western Rattlesnakes, Gopher Snakes, Racers and Striped Whipsnakes may den together in hibernation dens in eastern Oregon and Washington. Snakes usually converge on their hibernacula in early fall, and will spend days or even weeks basking outside on sunny days, but retreating into the den at night. In some species, mating may be initiated in the fall and continued in the spring. Pregnant female Western Rattlesnakes may give birth to their young at or near the den site, during this pre-hibernation period.

Emergence from hibernation varies considerably according to species and location, but in our area probably begins in late February or early March (some Garter Snakes), becomes common in late March and April, and may continue through May and into June in some eastern parts of our two states. Once out of the hibernaculum, most species of snakes disperse to their summer ranges, which can be up to a few miles away in some (e.g., Western Rattlesnake). Most snakes appear to have home ranges during their active season, within which they find adequate shelter and food. Whether or not they defend all or parts of these from others of their species is not well known. All snakes are carnivorous feeders, utilizing food items such as small insects and their larvae, larger insects, other invertebrates, and young and adults of fish, amphibians, reptiles, birds and mammals. It probably goes without saying that what a snake eats depends to a

large extent on its size, and generally larger snakes eat larger food items.
Snakes may tend to feed mainly on certain groups; for example, Common
Kingsnakes feed to a large extent on other snakes, including rattlesnakes, and
Ringneck Snakes feed on small snakes and lizards, but neither species utilizes
these foods exclusively. Some authorities believe that Sharptail Snakes feed
almost entirely on small slugs. Northwestern Garter Snakes eat a lot of earthworms and slugs, whereas Common Garter Snakes eat a wide variety of small
vertebrates, especially amphïbians.

Small or helpless food items may simply be grasped and swallowed,
whereas larger prey is killed or rendered helpless first, either by constriction,
which suffocates the victim, or by injection of a venom. Neurotoxic venoms kill
rapidly and the snake usually retains a grip on its victim until it dies.
Hemotoxins act slowly and snakes like rattlesnakes strike and envenomate their
prey, following which they withdraw and wait for an interval, then trail the
animal by means of their tongue and vomeronasal organs. It is probable that the
chemical trail they follow is a combination of the animal's scent and the scent of
the snake's venom. This would enable them to ignore the trails of healthy
animals, not yet bitten.

Snakes are ectothermic, requiring external heat sources to raise body
temperatures to preferred activity levels. They either expose all or part of the
body to sunlight (basking or heliothermy) or acquire heat from a warm substrate
(thigmothermy). Snakes tend to be considerably more thigmothermic than
lizards, a fact which often leads them to rest on sun-warmed blacktop or
concrete roads in the evening. This is a major source of snake fatalities in many
areas, especially where auto traffic is heavy. Drivers either fail to see the
snakes, or sad to say, run over them deliberately. Daytime temperatures at
ground level can be quite high during summer days, especially in desert areas,
causing many snakes to be active at night (e.g., Gopher Snake and Western
Rattlesnake), although they may be diurnal on cooler or less sunny days. Night
Snakes, as the name implies are almost always nocturnal, while Racers and
Striped Whipsnakes are usually diurnal.

Courtship and Reproduction

Many observers of snakes in past years occasionally saw what they
labeled as a sort of "dancing" between male and female snakes. It often involved a rearing up of the head and forepart of the body of each snake, followed
by a twining of their raised bodies or shoving of one another. It appeared as
though the snakes were not injuring one another but were simply trying to
wrestle one another into submission. As more careful observations were carried
out in later years, it became evident that the participants in the "dances" were
always males of the same species, often observed by a female of that species.
The phenomenon has been seen among many different species of snakes,
including Striped Whipsnakes, Gopher Snakes and Western Rattlesnakes.
Apparently, it is a ritualized combat in which the snakes are not trying to kill

each other, but are determining which snake is stronger and therefore the "fittest" in an evolutionary sense. If females then choose to mate with the winner of such contests, sexual selection is occurring, whereby the stronger male passes on his genes. It may also be that some instances of these contests are involved with territorial disputes, but this is uncertain.

Courtship and mating of Northwestern snakes usually occurs from late March into May, depending on location. During this season, females that are physiologically ready for mating leave a scent trail as they move about. The scent is probably a combination of glands opening adjacent to the cloaca and substances released by the developing egg yolks within her. Males encountering such a trail are able to follow it with frequent tongue flicks, and will eventually encounter the female. When a female is reached, most male snakes attempt to rub their chins along her back. Sensitive tubercles on the chin may stimulate both the male and the female during this rubbing. The male increasingly tries to align his body along that of the female, often twisting about her or throwing loops of his body across hers as they lie side by side. Eventually, the female opens her cloacal vent, allowing the male to insert one of his paired hemipenes into the cloaca. The hemipenis is everted (turned inside out) from the base of the male's tail out through the cloaca. The everted and enlarged organ is equipped with papillae and hooks which help to keep it in the female's cloaca during copulation. Sperm-containing semen flows along grooves or openings in the hemipenis and may be stored within the female for weeks or months before fertilizing the eggs.

Snakes are either oviparous (egg-laying) or viviparous (eggs retained in the body and young born alive). Among Northwestern snakes, the Rubber Boa, all Garter Snakes, and the Western Rattlesnake are viviparous, the remaining species being oviparous. Viviparity may enable snakes to inhabit cooler areas as evidenced by some of our Garter Snake species at higher elevations. Oviparous snakes deposit their eggs in a variety of places, the necessary requirements being that they are protected and will receive enough heat to hatch. Some eastern snakes have been known to nest in rotting manure piles, where the heat of decay hatched the eggs. Several years ago, eggs and remains of eggs of four species of snakes (Ringneck Snake, Sharptail Snake, Racer and Gopher Snake) and one lizard (Southern Alligator Lizard) were found among rocks and soil below a long-unused road cut on an open grassy south slope near Corvallis, Oregon. Remains of Gopher Snake eggs, destroyed by a predator (possibly a Striped Skunk) were on a south slope with scattered trees north of Corvallis. They appeared to have been in a rodent burrow. Numbers of eggs or young, when known, are given in the species accounts; they range from three to nine among egg-layers and three or four to 25 among live-bearers, the higher numbers belonging to Garter Snakes. Common Garter Snakes have been known to produce 70 to 80 young in some areas!

Young snakes grow rapidly, and depending upon elevation, usually reach sexual maturity in two or three years. In a careful study of a Western Rattlesnake population in California, the snakes grew from a hatching length of 11 inches (280 mm) to 24 inches (610 mm) in two years and were almost 36 inches (914 mm) long in 50 months. Snakes in captivity have been known to live an exceptional 38 years (Boa Constrictor), but the records for captive longevity are much less for smaller snakes, ranging from 6 to 18 years. Such ages might be exceptional for wild snakes, but little is known about this.

Snakes and Humans

Certainly the greatest enemy of snakes throughout the more recent part of their existence has been mankind. In the prehistoric times of human existence in tropical areas, snakes were probably feared because many of them were poisonous. One school of thought today contends that this logical fear of snakes through many generations became fixed in human heredity and is now instinctive. Others would deny this, feeling that anyone can be educated away from fearing snakes. Whatever the case, a great many people today don't like snakes and this dislike varies from a simple aversion to a hysterical fear or an urge to kill all snakes.

Throughout most of human history, these negative attitudes toward snakes had little impact on snake populations; humans were relatively low in numbers whereas snakes had evolved for millions of years and were abundant and adapted to a wide variety of habitats. In other words, snakes had plenty of living space and the scattered humans had little effect on them. Eventually, humans spread into almost every livable part of the world and their increasing numbers began to require more and more of the habitats used by snakes. At the same time, various customs and religious ideas increased, some of them involving negative attitudes toward snakes. Witness the belief that Adam and Eve were banished from the Garden of Eden because of listening to a snake! It is now evident that increasing human populations are steadily hurting snake numbers. Loss of habitat increases yearly and is accompanied by such artifacts of mankind as paved roads and fast cars and other vehicles, intensive agriculture, urban sprawl, desertification of arid lands, deforestation of the tropics, pesticides, rattlesnake "roundups", general aversion to snakes, etc.

Readers of previous sections of this general discussion of snakes must now realize that there are many impressive and interesting facts about members of this group. Here we have an assemblage of so-called "cold-blooded" animals without any limbs, making it necessary for them to crawl about on their bellies, that has evolved very widely into all of the warmer and temperate parts of the earth. The over 2,700 species of snakes represents one of the most successful radiations of living land vertebrates. Their adaptations for living in habitats from subterranean to arboreal, and from deserts to jungles and marine waters are fascinating, as are their various means of acquiring food. Some knowledge of these facts about snakes should make them less fearful to us, especially in Oregon and Washington, where only one of our 15 species is poisonous (and that one is easily identified). Snakes continue to be a most interesting part of our fauna, but their days may be numbered without our educated help.

Mohave Black-collared Lizard habitat
(Harney County, Oregon)
Photo by William P. Leonard

SPECIES ACCOUNTS

Desert Horned Lizard
Photo by William P. Leonard

SNAPPING TURTLE

Chelydra serpentina (Linnaeus)   {Introduced}

Description:

S napping Turtles **have large heads and limbs, causing the carapace to look proportionately small**, and giving them a somewhat prehistoric appearance. The **tail is thick and long** (usually longer than half the length of the shell) and the **dorsal edge is jagged with a row of enlarged scales. The posterior edge of the carapace is serrated, and the plastron is small and narrow.** Snapping Turtles **can reach large sizes**, going up to 18.6 inches (470 mm) in shell length and 75 pounds (34 kg) in weight.

Distribution:

Snapping Turtles are native to eastern North America and have been introduced at various sites in Washington and Oregon. Snapping Turtles have been found in Washington, around Lake Washington in Seattle (Sandpoint), in Bellevue and in the Puget Sound area (Yelm Highway). The turtle at Sandpoint was a female in the act of depositing 78 eggs in a nest! In Oregon, snappers have been caught near Portland, Corvallis, Springfield and Coos Bay, and observed in a pond northeast of Roseburg. How this species became so wide-spread is a puzzle, because Snapping Turtles are rarely sold in pet stores. However, they grow fast and bite quite readily, so owners may dispose of them once they reach a large size.

Habits and Habitat:

Snapping Turtles usually prefer quiet waters with muddy bottoms and much vegetation, but in their native range, they occur in a broad spectrum of habitats, from brackish waters along the east coast to foothill streams of the Rocky Mountains. They rarely leave the water to bask and often hide during daylight hours, which makes detection difficult in nature. When captured, they will attempt to bite and can inflict a severe wound because of their large size. Number of eggs per clutch ranges from 10 to 83, but is usually 20 to 30. Females appear to lay one clutch per year, but some may have two clutches within a year.

Adult (Schoolcraft
County, Michigan)

Photo by William P. Leonard

Adult (Ingham County,
Michigan)

Photo by James H. Harding

Plastron (Michigan)

Photo by James H. Harding

PAINTED TURTLE
Chrysemys picta (Schneider)

Description:

T he Painted Turtle is distinctively marked with an **olive-gray or blackish-green carapace, a reddish plastron and yellow or thin reddish stripes on the neck and legs**. Carapace (dorsal shell) of adults 4-9 inches (127-229 mm) long; hatchlings are about one inch (25.4 mm) in shell length. The carapace is low and broad, generally widest behind its middle, and in adults smooth and lacks a keel or serrations. Males may have a concave plastron, which is not true of females. The cloacal vent in males is posterior to the edge of the carapace, but in females the vent is located more anteriorly. The males have longer front claws than females.

Similar Species:

In the Western Pond Turtle, the dorsal color is dark brown or dull olive (with or without darker reticulations or streaking) and the plastron is yellowish (sometimes with dark markings in the centers of the scutes). Slider turtles (an introduced species) often have a bright red stripe behind the eye, broad yellow stripes on the legs and neck, bright yellow plastron and green to dark green carapace. Some sliders are melanistic (black) as adults.

Distribution:

Painted Turtles range from the Columbia Gorge eastward, and are most abundant in the Columbia River Basin east of the Cascade Mountains. A few records occur in the Puget Sound region of Washington and south to near Salem in the Willamette Valley, Oregon. This turtle has been introduced widely in the Pacific Northwest. They occur from sea level to about 3,000 feet (915 m).

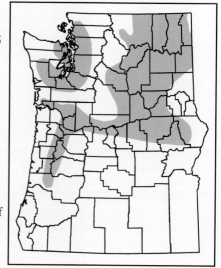

Habits and Habitat:

The Painted Turtle frequents marshes, slow rivers, ponds and lakes, and they concentrate in slow waters with large amounts of aquatic vegetation. They often congregate on logs or branches to bask, and become aggressive toward each other when crowded. Painted Turtles also may bask on top of aquatic vegetation, and dive into mats of plants when disturbed.

30

Adult (Columbia National Wildlife Refuge, Washington)
Photo by William R. Radke

Close-up of an adult (Okanogan County, Washington)
Photo by William P. Leonard

The Painted Turtle is omnivorous and foods include insects, other arthropods, crayfish, tadpoles and almost all aquatic plants. Individuals grow slowly in the wild, and age of first reproduction is about 5-6 years in females, but 3-4 years in males. Females produce 4-20 eggs per clutch, averaging about 8 eggs per year. Females appear to deposit one clutch every year and the nests are generally in sandy soil or grassy areas near water.

Remarks:

The Painted Turtle appears to be stable in numbers throughout most of its range, but can be exploited for the pet trade. Few turtles are known in the Puget Sound region, but this may be natural because the species is at the westernmost edge of its range. There are four subspecies of the Painted Turtle, but only the Western Painted Turtle (*Chrysemys picta bellii*) occurs in the Northwest.

Adult (Okanogan
County, Washington)

Photo by William P. Leonard

Plastron (Okanogan
County, Washington)

Photo by William P. Leonard

Dorsal view of adult
(Turnbull National
Wildlife Refuge,
Washington)

Photo by Charles R. Peterson

WESTERN POND TURTLE
Clemmys marmorata (Baird and Girard)

Description:

T he dorsal color is usually **dark brown or dull olive**, with or without darker reticulations or streaking. The **plastron is yellowish, sometimes with dark blotches in the centers of the scutes.** The shell is 4.5 to 8.25 inches (110-210 mm) long. Hatchlings are about one inch (25.4 mm) in shell length. The dorsal shell (carapace) is low and broad, usually widest behind the middle, and in adults is smooth, lacking a keel or serrations. Adult Western Pond Turtles are sexually dimorphic as follows: Males have a light or pale yellow throat, a concave plastron, and the cloacal vent is at or posterior to the edge of the carapace, whereas females have a brownish throat with dark flecking, a more convex plastron and the cloacal vent is within the posterior edge of the carapace.

Similar Species:

The Painted Turtle is distinctively marked with an olive-grey or blackish-green carapace, a reddish plastron and yellow or thin reddish stripes on the neck and legs. Sliders often have a broad red stripe behind the eye, broad yellow stripes on the legs and neck, a bright yellow plastron and a green to dark green carapace.

Distribution:

Western Pond Turtles originally ranged from northern Baja California, Mexico, north to the Puget Sound region of Washington, but in recent years they have become rare or absent in the Puget Sound area. They have a disjunct distribution in most of the Northwest, and some isolated populations exist is southern Washington. Pond Turtles are now rare in the Willamette Valley north of Eugene, Oregon, but abundance increases south of that city where temperatures are higher. They may be locally common in some streams, rivers and ponds in southern Oregon. A few records are reported east of the Cascade Mountains, but these may have been based on introduced individuals. They range up to 1,000 feet (305 m) in Washington, and to about 3,000 feet (915 m) in Oregon.

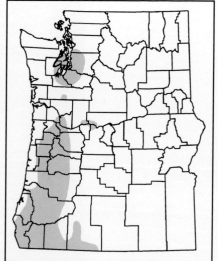

Adult male (Lane County, Oregon)
Photo by John S. Applegarth

Basking adult (Klickitat County, Washington)
Photo by Kate Slavens

Habits and Habitat:

The Western Pond Turtle occurs in both permanent and intermittent waters, including marshes, streams, rivers, ponds and lakes. They favor habitats with large amounts of emergent logs or boulders, where they aggregate to bask. Individuals display aggressive behavior toward one another while sunning. They also bask on top of aquatic vegetation or position themselves just below the surface where water temperatures are elevated. During aerial basking, the Western Pond Turtle seems to be more alert than the Painted Turtle. Western Pond Turtles will rapidly dive off basking sites when approached by a human, even at distances of over 50 m. Consequently, this species is often overlooked in the wild. However, it is possible to observe resident turtles by moving slowly and hiding behind shrubs and trees.

Western Pond Turtles are omnivorous and most of their animal diet includes insects, crayfish and other aquatic invertebrates. Fishes, tadpoles and frogs are eaten occasionally, and carrion is eaten when available. Plant foods include filamentous algae, lily pods, and tule and cattail roots.

Females produce 5-13 eggs per clutch; some may deposit eggs only every other year, while others produce two clutches in a year. They may travel some distance from water for egg-laying, moving as much as 1/2 mile (0.8 km) away from and up to 300 feet (90 m) above the nearest source of water, but most nests are within 100 yards (90 m) of water. The female usually leaves the water in the evening and may wander far before selecting a nest site, often in an open area of sand or hardpan that is facing southward. The nest is flask-shaped with an opening of about two inches (50 mm). Females spend considerable time covering up the nest with soil and adjacent low vegetation, making it difficult for a person to find unless it has been disturbed by a predator.

Some hatchlings overwinter in the nest, and this phenomenon seems more prevalent in northern areas. Possibly, winter rains may be necessary to loosen the hardpan soil where some nests are deposited. Whether it is hatchlings or eggs that overwinter, young first appear in the spring following the year of egg deposition. Individuals grow slowly in the wild, and age of first reproduction may be 10 to 12 years in the northern part of the range. Adult turtles may survive more than 30 years in the wild.

Remarks:

The Western Pond Turtle appears to be declining in numbers, particularly in the northernmost part of its range. Few turtles persist in the Seattle and general Puget Sound region. Only small populations are known in and north of the Willamette Valley, Oregon. They are more common in large river basins in southern Oregon. Threats to native turtles include habitat alteration, predation on young turtles by exotic Bullfrogs and fishes, drought, local disease outbreaks and fragmentation of remaining populations. Rangewide, the Western Pond Turtle is under consideration for listing as a threatened species. The turtle is protected by Oregon and Washington.

Plastron of male (left)
and female (right)
(Oregon)

Photo by Michael J. Adams

Hatchling (Washington)

Photo by Kate Slavens

Adult (Klickitat County,
Washington)

Photo by Kate Slavens

SLIDER

Trachemys scripta (Schoepff)   {Introduced}

Description:

S liders are **moderate in size, with the shell up to 10.5 inches (268 mm) long**. They have a **bright-colored patch behind the eye, varying from a broad red stripe in the Red-eared Slider (*T. s. elegans*) to a yellow blotch in the Yellow-bellied Turtle (*T. s. scripta*).** Other subspecies of the Slider rarely occur in the West. A Slider has yellow stripes on the legs and neck, a bright yellow plastron and a green to dark green carapace, streaked with yellow and black. Old adults may become melanistic, which makes them difficult to tell apart from our native species (except that Red-ears retain the distinct red stripe).

Distribution:

Sliders occur naturally from eastern North America to northernmost South America. They are the most common turtle sold in pet stores, resulting in some being released, so that now sliders are both widespread and common in Pacific Northwest waters. For example, one of us (Bury) recorded a minimum of 16 Sliders at American and Sequalitchew Lakes at Fort Lewis, Washington. He observed one juvenile about 3 inches (76 mm) long in American Lake and caught three Sliders by hand or dip net: a 5 inch (127 mm) sub-adult male, a 5 inch (127 mm) sub-adult female, and a 5.6 inch (143 mm) female.

Habits and Habitat:

Sliders frequent ponds, lakes and other quiet waters. They usually reach their highest numbers in shallow lakes or lake margins with mud bottoms and dense vegetation. They bask on logs or other emergent objects for many hours each day during warm weather. They are an omnivore, but switch mostly to plant material as they become larger. The number of eggs per female increases with her size. The mean clutch size is about 8 eggs at a 7.9 inch (200 mm) carapace length and 13 eggs at a 10.2 inch (260 mm) carapace length. Some females may deposit more than one clutch per year while other females (about half of one population in South Carolina) are not reproductively active each year.

Remarks:

Observations of egg-laying by adult females include the Puget Sound area, near Portland, Oregon, and southern Oregon. However, we lack information on their fecundity (e.g., clutch size or number of adult females with eggs) and survivorship of young in the Pacific Northwest. The high frequency of occurrence and numbers of sliders now present in Northwest waters suggest that self-sustaining populations are well-established regionally.

Close-up showing red
"ears" (Michigan)

Photo by James H. Harding

Adult (Lake County,
Tennesee)

Photo by James H. Harding

Plastron of an adult
(Michigan)

Photo by James H. Harding

LOGGERHEAD
Caretta caretta (Linnaeus)

Description:

This moderate-sized sea turtle has **five pairs of costal scutes** on the carapace with the **nuchal scute touching the first costal.** There are **three large scutes (inframaginals) on the bridge; these lack pores.** The carapace is reddish-brown and the plastron is yellow or cream. The common name refers to the large head, the coloration of which is reddish or chestnut to olive-brown with yellow margins on the head scales.

When mature, the Loggerhead measures about 3.3 to 4 feet (1 to 1.2 m) in carapace length and 220 to 330 pounds (100-150 kg) in weight. A few are larger with one record to 992 pounds (450 kg).

Distribution:

Juvenile Loggerheads of carapace length 30 to 60 cm are found on the Pacific Coast of North America, but adults are not. As a species Loggerheads occur in subtropical and temperate waters in all major oceans. Seasonally they occur in waters off Washington and Oregon during late summer and occasionally wash ashore or are seen offshore.

Habits and Habitat:

The large head packs powerful musculature and jaws, used for feeding on hard-shelled crustaceans and mollusks. The diet includes many other items, such as sponges, clams, conchs, squid and seaweed. They eat fish, but it is not known if these are taken as carrion or caught. Nesting occurs on beaches in subtropical waters. Females nest every two or three years and deposit up to 120 eggs in multiple clutches (maximum of seven in one season).

Remarks:

The Loggerhead is recognized as a Federal Threatened species. In Pacific waters, they may die in longlines (most frequently caught species in Hawaiian longline fishery) and in nets. Shrimp trawlers in the southeastern U.S. drowned many in the past, but excluder devices (basically a trap door) now enable turtles to escape nets.

Juvenile
Photo by Scott A. Eckert

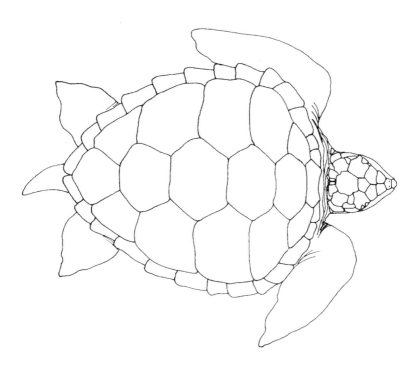

GREEN TURTLE
Chelonia mydas (Linnaeus)

Description:

This large sea turtle has **four pairs of costal scutes** on the carapace and the **nuchal scute does not touch the first costal.** The relatively small head has a single pair of prefrontal scales and a serrated upper and lower jaw. The scales on the head often have yellow or pale margins. The species name derives from internal greenish fat bodies, and the external body color is quite variable. The skin is brown to black while the carapace is usually gray-green or olive and the plastron yellow or pale. Green Turtles reach 5 feet (1.5 m) in carapace length and 110 to 300 pounds (50-136 kg) in weight.

Distribution:

This species frequents tropical and subtropical waters of the Atlantic and Pacific oceans. Some range as far north as Alaska, and an occasional Green Turtle occurs off Washington and Oregon beaches. They usually appear during periods of warm oceanic conditions in summer. Green Turtles reside year around in the bays around San Diego and in the cooling water outfalls of power generating facilities on the southern California coast.

Habits and Habitat:

The Green Turtle nests on beaches in tropical and subtropical regions (e.g., Hawaii and the Pacific Coast of Mexico). Females nest every two or three years, but have multiple clutches in those years of nesting. Clutch sizes are 100-150 eggs, deposited two to three weeks apart.

Remarks:

Green Turtles that occur along the west coast of North America may nest in Hawaii or Mexico; we currently do not know their origins in our waters. In some tropical waters, the eggs and meat of Green Turtles are still taken for human consumption. Some adults are caught in gill nets or hit by high speed boats.

Adult (Galapagos Islands, Ecuador)
Photo by Peter Pritchard

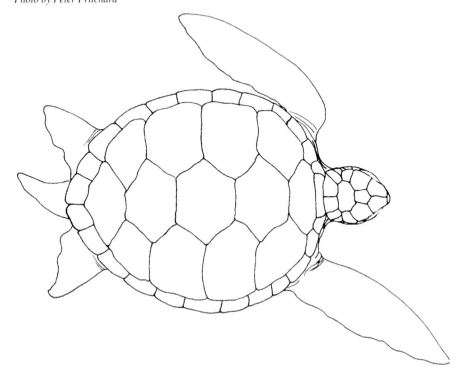

PACIFIC RIDLEY
Lepidochelys olivacea (Eschscholtz)

Description:

This relatively small sea turtle has **six pairs of costal scutes** (may range from five to nine) and the **nuchal touches the first costal.** There are **four large inframarginal scutes on the bridge, each of which has a single pore posteriorly.** The carapace is generally olive while the plastron and bridges are light greenish or yellow. As mature turtles they exhibit a high, flat-topped, domed carapace. As juveniles the posterior edges of the carapace are serrated and they may also have raised ridges down the vertebral and costal scutes. Pacific Ridleys grow to about 2.5 feet (0.8 m) and 80 to 100 pounds (36-45 kg).

Distribution:

Pacific Ridleys occur mostly in tropical waters in the Pacific and Indian Oceans. They are a rarity in waters off Washington and Oregon.

Habits and Habitat:

This turtle is carnivorous and foods include crabs, conchs and fish; they may eat some seaweed. Nesting occurs on tropical beaches. Females nest every two or three years and deposit 30 to 170 eggs in two or three clutches per season. Some females may nest annually while others deposit eggs every other year.

Remarks:

The Pacific Ridley is listed as Federal Threatened across most of its range and as Endangered for the populations nesting along the Pacific side of Mexico. In the past, many eggs were taken for food and the adults were used for food and leather. Many of these activities are now prohibited or reduced, but enforcement is difficult. Many wild stocks are depleted.

Adult
Photo by Scott A. Eckert

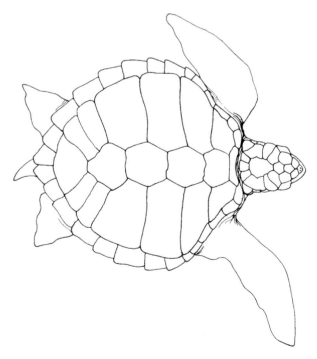

LEATHERBACK

Dermochelys coriacea (Linnaeus)

Description:

T he Leatherback is the **only sea turtle with a smooth skin** (leather), which is also saturated with oil. **There are seven keels running the length of the carapace, long front flippers lack claws and the shell is elongated.** The head, neck, flippers and shell are brown to black, sometimes with whitish spots. The plastron is white or pale in color. Leatherbacks are the largest of all sea turtles, reaching 8 feet (2.4 m) in carapace length and weights of 1,600 pounds (725 kg). One record turtle weighed 2,017 pounds (915 kg).

Distribution:

Leatherbacks range widely across the tropics and subtropics, and seasonally migrate into Arctic and Antarctic waters. They occur off the coasts of Washington and Oregon. Leatherbacks are pelagic, generally swimming far offshore, but occasionally will enter bays and estuaries. When one of these behemoths dies and washes ashore, there often is a flurry of news attention, because these turtles are huge reptiles.

Habits and Habitat:

Leatherbacks can retain body heat because of their large body size, an oil-dense skin (an insulation layer) and counter current blood circulation systems in the limbs. These adaptations permit Leatherbacks to inhabit cooler seas than other sea turtles. Biologists have recorded elevated body temperatures of Leatherbacks at 25°-26° C in cool seas (8° C) and 30°-31° C in warm waters (28° C). Leatherbacks can dive to 4,250 feet (1,295 m) and reach speeds in water of up to 4.5 miles/hour (9 km/hour). Leatherbacks do not (intentionally) eat anything but jellyfish.

Nesting beaches are in subtropical and tropical areas. Females deposit about 100 eggs (range 50-170) in each of several clutches per season. Like most sea turtles, Leatherback females nest every other year or at longer intervals.

Remarks:

This is a Federal Endangered species, and fully protected in U.S. waters. However, eggs are taken for food in the tropics. Some Leatherbacks are killed when caught in longlines used for fishing in the open ocean. They swallow plastic bags and other oceanic debris that resemble jellyfish and the debris can block the intestinal tract and cause death.

Adult
Photo by Scott A. Eckert

Adult
Photo by Scott A. Eckert

NORTHERN ALLIGATOR LIZARD
Elgaria coerulea (Wiegmann)

Description:

A brown to dark brown or greenish brown lizard, **showing a longitudinal fold on each side of the body** which identifies it as an alligator lizard. There is usually a row of dark spots down the mid-dorsal area and the squarish dorsal scales are separated from the similar ventral scales by an area of very small scales beneath the lateral fold. With the exception of some of the Siskiyou Mountains members of this species, there are no white-tipped black scales on the sides (see below). **Faint dark lines run down the edges of the ventral scale rows. The eyes are brown.** Juveniles show a coppery dorsal stripe, with or without dark central spots. Northern Alligator Lizards are seldom more than 4 inches (100 mm) in snout-vent length and range up to 10 inches (254 mm) in total length.

Similar Species:

Differs from all of our other lizards, except the Southern Alligator Lizard, in having a lateral fold on each side of the trunk. Differs from the Southern Alligator Lizard by having dark lines down the edges of the ventral scale rows rather than down the middle of each row, and by having brown eyes (versus yellow).

Distribution:

From Vancouver Island and southern British Columbia south through western Washington and Oregon into the northern Coast Range and Sierras of California. Also, from British Columbia across northeastern Washington into northern Idaho and extreme northwestern Montana. Occurs throughout most of western Washington and Oregon, except absent from much of the coastal area of Washington and from the open valley floors of western Oregon. Occurs up to at least 6,000 feet (1,830 m) in the Cascades of Oregon and to 4,620 feet (1,409 m) at Bear Lake, Yakima County in Washington. Also occurs in the Okanogan Highlands (Okanogan County), in extreme northeastern Washington, and there are isolated populations on Hart Mountain and in the Warner Mountains of eastern Oregon.

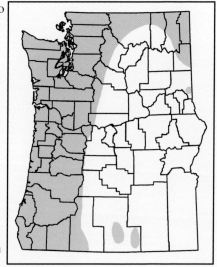

Adult showing brown eye (Thurston County, Washington)
Photo by William P. Leonard

Adult (Siskiyou County, California)
Photo by John S. Applegarth

Habits and Habitat:

Northern Alligator Lizards usually occur in more moist and cooler habitats than do Southern Alligator Lizards, including forests and forest clearings. It is the only lizard that occurs along the coast north of Coos County, in Oregon. In the western part of their range in our area, their distribution tends to complement that of the Southern Alligator Lizard. Within forested habitats, Northern Alligator Lizards require openings for foraging and basking. They feed mainly on insects and other small invertebrates.

Mating occurs in April at lower elevations and as late as June in the mountains. The eggs are retained in the body of the female until fully-developed young are born about three months later, between July and early September. A female captured in the North Cascades of Washington gave birth to five young over a two-day period (Sept. 21 and 22), the newborns averaging just under 3 inches (74 mm) in total length. Clutch size is usually three to eight. This live-bearing phenomenon probably allows the species to occupy cooler areas since the female can continually move herself and the eggs within her to appropriate sunny basking spots throughout the day.

Northern Alligator Lizards seem able to operate at cooler temperatures than other lizards. They have been seen swimming in cool streams and one individual has been encountered foraging on a wet rock face during a dark rainy night. In the Coast Range of Oregon, this species hibernates in cavities within large logs or cracks and in crevices within sandstone or mudstone outcrops.

Remarks:

There are four subspecies of *Elgaria coerulea*, but only two occur in the Northwest. *Elgaria coerulea principis*, the Northwestern Alligator Lizard, is the most widespread, being found in most of the species range within our area. It is replaced in southwestern Oregon by *Elgaria coerulea shastensis*, the Shasta Alligator Lizard, which differs from *principis* in being larger (to about 5 inches or 130 mm snout-vent), in having 16 scale rows (versus 14) and in being highly variable in coloration. Many Shasta individuals have gray heads with yellowish or tan bodies heavily marked with black crossbands. Some have white-tipped black scales on the sides of the trunk, whereas others don't. In addition, intergrades between the two subspecies are present to further confuse one. Finally, some *shastensis* have no faint dark lines on the abdomen and are difficult to place in this species. There is an obvious need for further studies of this subspecies.

Adult (Thurston County, Washington)

Photo by William P. Leonard

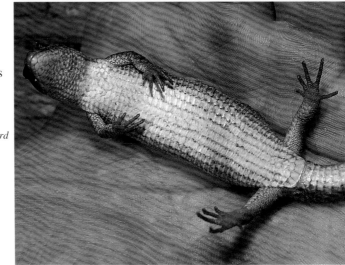

Ventral scales dark along the lateral edges (Thurston County, Washington)

Photo by William P. Leonard

Juvenile (Thurston County, Washington)

Photo by William P. Leonard

SOUTHERN ALLIGATOR LIZARD
Elgaria multicarinata (Blainville)

Description:

T his large lizard is recognizable as an alligator lizard by the presence of a **lateral fold on each side of the body between the front and rear legs.** Squarish scales on dorsal and ventral surfaces are separated by much smaller scales beneath the lateral fold. The dorsal color is usually brown or olive-brown with dusky wavy lines across the trunk and onto the tail. The sides show vertical lines of white-tipped black scales. **The ventral color is gray with faint longitudinal lines running down the centers of the scale rows. The eyes are yellow.**

Juveniles lack the dark cross lines on the back, appearing to have a wide coppery stripe running the length of the back and onto the tail. Southern Alligator Lizards range in size up to 5.5 inches (140 mm) in snout-vent length and 11.5 inches (292 mm) in total length.

Similar Species:

With the exception of the Northern Alligator Lizard, none of our other lizards shows a lateral fold. Northern Alligator Lizards have brown eyes and the dark ventral lines run along the edges of the scale rows.

Distribution:

From south-central Washington and north-central Oregon through western Oregon to the coast mountains and valleys of western California into northern Baja California. In Washington, occurs along the Columbia River in Skamania and Klickitat Counties, ranging north through eastern Yakima County to southern Kittitas County. Found in interior valleys and foothill regions of western Oregon; extends up the Columbia Gorge and then up the Deschutes and John Day Rivers to northern Deschutes County and western Grant County respectively. Occurs from 400 feet (121 m) near Lyle, Klickitat County, to 3,182 feet (971 m) near Satus Pass, Klickitat County, Washington. In Oregon, probably occurs to 3,000 feet (914 m) in the southwestern part of the state.

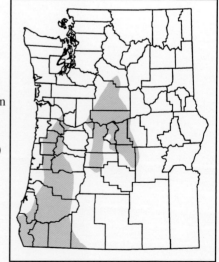

Adult (Klickitat County, Washington)
Photo by Kate Slavens

Adult showing yellow eye (Jackson County, Oregon)
Photo by William P. Leonard

Habits and Habitat:

This species prefers oak woodland and chaparral vegetation, characteristic of Coast Range foothills and of most of the valleys and hills in southwestern Oregon. In the Columbia Gorge and distributions to the east, they frequent brushy stabilized talus areas and oak woodlands where these occur. Southern Alligator Lizards are active during the day, hunting a variety of insects and other arthropods, and have been known to feed on bird eggs and some small mammals. They are secretive and difficult to spot as they slip more or less quietly through brushy cover. When moving rapidly, Southern Alligator Lizards press their legs against the body and undulate their bodies in snake-like fashion. They may climb into bushes or small trees, where the tail can be used to grasp branches. These lizards will not hesitate to bite when handled (a painful experience).

Mating probably occurs during April and May and eggs are placed in rodent burrows or talus crevices in mid-summer. An Oregon female brought in on July 24 laid 14 elliptical eggs on August 3. In nature, hatching occurs in September or early October, producing young measuring a little over an inch (30 mm) in snout-vent length. Juveniles and adults usually hibernate from some time in November into March.

Remarks:

The species, *Elgaria multicarinata*, includes five subspecies throughout its range but only *E. m. scincicauda*, the Oregon Alligator Lizard, occurs in our area. Because of its preference for woodlands and brushy areas, this species may be encountered in suburban yards.

Adult (Klickitat
County, Washington)

Photo by William P. Leonard

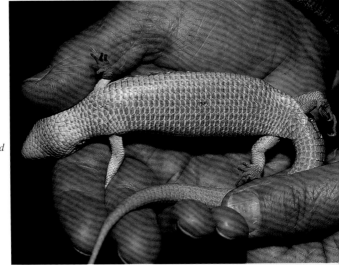

Ventral scales light
colored along lateral
and posterior edges
(Jackson County,
Oregon)

Photo by William P. Leonard

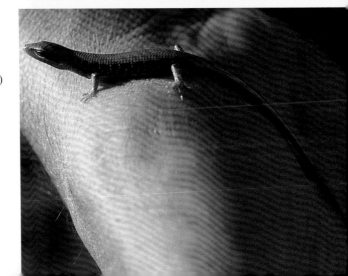

Juvenile (Klickitat
County, Washington)

Photo by Kate Slavens

MOJAVE BLACK-COLLARED LIZARD

Crotaphytus bicinctores   Smith and Tanner

Description:

This large colorful lizard is **recognizable by its two distinct black dorsal collars, separated by a light collar.** The **head appears large** and is separated from the body by a distinct neck. The **gray, tan or reddish back shows sometimes barely visible alternating lighter and darker crossbands,** and is usually liberally sprinkled with small light spots. The entire pattern may appear very dark on cool mornings. The long tail is somewhat laterally compressed and heavily spotted. **Male Mojave Black-collared Lizards possess a large blue-black to black throat patch** and appear to have larger heads than females. A large male, perched on a hillside boulder, is a most colorful and impressive sight. **Females are smaller than males, lack the dark throat and are marked with narrow vertical orange bands on the sides during the breeding season.** Both sexes often appear to have pale yellow gloves on front and rear feet. Males may range up to 4.3 inches (109 mm) in snout-vent length and to near 12.9 inches (328 mm) in total length.

Similar Species:

No other lizard in our area shows the pattern of two black dorsal collars separated by a light collar.

Distribution:

Southeastern Oregon and southwestern Idaho south through western Nevada, western and southern Utah, and extreme northwestern Arizona to southeastern California and Baja California. In our area, limited to southeastern Oregon in southern Harney County and the Owyhee drainage of Malheur County. They occur to at least 5,000 feet (1,524 m) in some canyons south of Fields, Harney County.

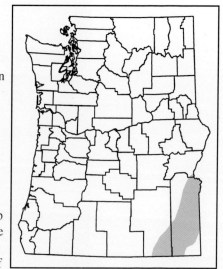

Habits and Habitat:

Mojave Black-collared Lizards are inhabitants of boulder hillsides, rock piles and talus slopes at the bases of cliffs. They are limited in climbing ability and avoid large rocks with steep sides, as well as cliff faces. On hillside habitats, vegetation is usually sparse and short. One can stand at the base of

Adult male (Harney County, Oregon)
Photo by William P. Leonard

Adult male (Harney County)
Photo by William P. Leonard

a rocky hillside and spot basking Collared Lizards with binoculars.

Mojave Black-collared Lizards emerge from hibernation in late April or May. After emergence, males defend territories, and chases and limited fights are common. Each individual male overlooks his territory from an elevation within it, usually a sizable rock. When running at full speed, Collared Lizards use only the rear feet.

Little is known of the reproductive habits of this species in the Northwest. Elsewhere, they are thought to deposit one or two clutches of three to eight eggs in loose soil or in rodent burrows. It is probable that only one clutch is produced in our area, and newly hatched juveniles can be seen in late August and early September. The young measure about 1.4 inches (36 mm) in snout-vent length. Mojave Black-collared Lizards are known to feed on insects and other inverte- brates, as well as lizards, small snakes, flowers and tender vegetation.

Although quite wary much of the time, Collared Lizards often tolerate a close approach if one is careful. They may display by raising up on all four legs and compressing themselves laterally to appear larger. If pressed too closely, they retreat to the other side of their rock or boulder. They are capable of a painful bite if handled carelessly. As with other desert lizards, Mojave Black- collared Lizards do poorly in captivity and should not be captured.

Adult female (Harney County, Oregon)

Photo by William P. Leonard

Adult (Harney County, Oregon)

Photo by William P. Leonard

Adult shedding (Harney County, Oregon)

Photo by William P. Leonard

Long-nosed Leopard Lizard
Gambelia wislizenii (Baird and Girard)

Description:

This large, long-tailed lizard varies in the lightness or darkness of its ground color according to its temperature. On cool mornings, it may be quite dark and show best the **narrow light lines crossing the back of the body. These lines are usually offset along the mid-dorsal area.** At warmer temperatures, the light tannish ground color contrasts with dark **dorsal rounded or angular spots, which tend to form two longitudinal lines on each side of the body.** The spots extend onto the tail as two rows which may merge to form bars distally. The **underside is white with grayish stripes on the throat. Mature females exhibit spots of vivid orange or reddish-orange on the sides of the head and body, and a solid area of the same color on the underside of the tail during the breeding season (late May through June).**

Juvenile Long-nosed Leopard Lizards are large-headed with obvious light lines across the back, separated by dark areas with a rusty-reddish tinge. Dorsal scales on lizards of all ages are small and granular. The tail is rounded in cross-section. Females are larger than males, being up to 4.6 inches (116 mm) in snout-vent length and to 13 inches (331 mm) in total length, whereas males are usually less than 3.9 inches (100 mm) in snout-vent length and 11.9 inches (309 mm) in total length.

Similar Species:

Long-nosed Leopard Lizards are unique among northwestern lizards in having a combination of granular dorsal scales, light transverse lines and dark spots on the back and a rounded tail.

Distribution:

From southeastern Oregon and southern Idaho south into Baja California and northern Mexico. In Oregon, they occur in eastern and southern Malheur County, southern Harney County and at a few localities in southern Lake County. There are old records from The Dalles, Wasco County and Hat Rock, Morrow County. The Wasco County population is now extinct and the survival of the Morrow County one is dubious. They range to about 4,800 feet (1,463 m) in southern Harney County.

Adult male (Harney County, Oregon)
Photo by William P. Leonard

Adult female (Harney County, Oregon)
Photo by William P. Leonard

Habits and Habitat:

These are lizards of relatively flat desert areas, where the sandy to gravelly soil is grown to scattered shrubs. Grass or herbaceous growth between the shrubs is usually scant or absent. Leopard Lizards rely on rodent burrows for cover but are capable of digging their own.

Courtship and mating occur in late May and early June, at which time females develop their orange coloration. Four to seven eggs are deposited during June in burrows dug by the female, and hatching occurs one and one-half to two months later, usually during August or early September. The newly-hatched young are about 1.6 inches (40 mm) in snout-vent length.

Leopard Lizards usually emerge from their burrows between 8:00 and 9:00 AM on summer mornings and may be quite dark at that time. After emergence they sit with the back arched and toward the sun in order to gain maximum warmth. The lizards are least active in early afternoon (about 1:00 to 3:00 PM) and become more active in late afternoon, usually disappearing into burrows by 6:00 PM. During the hottest part of the summer, usually August, Leopard Lizards begin to leave the surface to aestivate, and may or may not re-appear in early September, prior to hibernation.

Long-nosed Leopard Lizards feed on a variety of insects and spiders, but are known to take small mammals (mice) and other lizards. Indicative of sharp eyesight, they feed by quietly watching for a victim then dashing to capture it. The lizards have a variety of behaviors to regulate their body temperature, including climbing into shrubbery to escape higher ground temperatures. When threatened, they open the mouth, exposing the black lining, and hiss or squeak quite audibly. These lizards do not last long in captivity and should not be captured.

Remarks:

There are two subspecies of the Long-nosed Leopard Lizard, but only the Large-spotted Leopard Lizard (*Gambelia wislizenii wislizenii*) occurs in our area.

Underside of a female (Harney County, Oregon)

Photo by William P. Leonard

Adult female (Harney County, Oregon)

Photo by William P. Leonard

Adult male (Harney County, Oregon)

Photo by William P. Leonard

SHORT-HORNED LIZARD
Phrynosoma douglassii (Bell)

Description:

T his **small lizard has a flat round body, edged with a single row of pointed scales on each side.** The "horns" are only **stubby scales at the back of the head** and are about as high as they are wide. The basic back color is usually some shade of gray to almost black, but may be brown or with reddish tones. **There are about twelve dark blotches on the back that tend to be arranged in transverse rows,** leaving the **central vertebral area unblotched.** Each blotch is edged posteriorly with a light color (white to pale yellow). The general color tends to match the color of the substrate of the area. The underside is white to light yellow and unspotted. Adults may reach a total length of 3.9 inches (100 mm), with a snout-vent length of 2.6 inches (66 mm), but most encountered are smaller.

Similar Species:

Distinguishable from all other lizards, except the Desert Horned, by its flat body, edged with a row of enlarged pointed scales. Desert Horned Lizards have a larger size and obvious long sharp horns. Juvenile Desert Horned Lizards have shorter horns than adults, but their horns are quite evident, whereas Short-horned Lizards appear to have no horns.

Distribution:

Western United States from extreme southern Canada south into north-central Mexico, west into eastern Washington, eastern Oregon and northern Nevada, and east into North and South Dakota, Nebraska, Colorado and New Mexico. Absent or scarce in the very northern part of eastern Washington. It ranges in Washington up to 2,200 feet (671 m) near Creston, Lincoln County. In Oregon, Short-horned Lizards occur in the Cascades of eastern Lane County and western Jefferson County and through central eastern Oregon, being absent from the easternmost counties. Ranges up to at least 5,000 feet (1,677 m) in the Oregon Cascades.

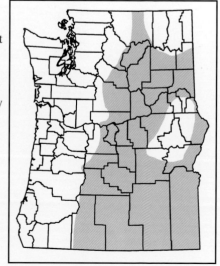

Habits and Habitat:

Short-horned Lizards range from the sagebrush plains of eastern Washington and Oregon into open juniper

Adult (Saddle Mountain National Wildlife Refuge, Washington)
Photo by William R. Radke

Juvenile (Grant County, Washington)
Photo by William P. Leonard

and pine woodlands adjacent to the Cascades. In the Oregon Cascades, they occur in open areas of volcanic soil and in pine woodlands. Whatever the general soil type (silty, sandy or gravelly), there must be spots of loose soil for burrowing. This species seldom occurs together with the Desert Horned Lizard, being able to occupy higher and cooler areas, a distribution probably related to their being live-bearing.

Depending on the area, Short-horned Lizards emerge from hibernation from late March into June. Mating occurs soon after emergence and the eggs are retained within the mother until live young are born about two months later (August to mid-September). In our area, females have three to fifteen young per year, with a Cascade Mountains female averaging about half the number of young produced by an eastern Oregon female. The newborn young measure from about 0.8 inches (20 mm) total length in the Oregon Cascades to near 1.25 inches (32 mm) total length in eastern Washington and Oregon.

During the heat of the summer, Short-horned Lizards are most active during the morning hours (prior to 11:00 AM), with lesser activity in late afternoon. They feed mainly on insects, particularly ants.

Remarks:

There are six subspecies of Short-horned Lizards, but only the Pigmy Short-horned Lizard (*Phrynosoma douglassii douglassii*) occurs in our area. The Cascade Mountains populations of this lizard differ in several ways from populations to the east, a situation needing further study. Short-horned Lizards are attractive and easily caught, but they only survive for a few weeks in captivity, and should be left alone.

Adult (Linn County, Oregon)

Photo by Robert M. Storm

Juvenile (Grant County, Oregon)

Photo by William P. Leonard

Adult buried in sand (Saddle Mountain N.W.R., Washington)

Photo by William R. Radke

DESERT HORNED LIZARD
Phrynosoma platyrhinos Girard

Description:

The body is very flattened with a row of pointed scales along the lateral edges. At the back of the head are two enlarged pointed scales (the horns) with smaller pointed scales lateral to these. The ground color is light tan to brown, gray or reddish, with gray to black wavy blotches across the back and tail. There is a large dark blotch on each side of the neck. The general color scheme tends to match well the colors of the substrate on which the lizard lives. The ventral color is white to light tan with scattered small spots. Adult Desert Horned Lizards reach about 5.5 inches (140 mm) in total length and 3.75 inches (95 mm) in snout-vent length, the tail being less than half the head and body length.

Similar Species:

No other Northwestern lizard possesses large pointed scales or horns at the rear edge of the head. The Short-horned Lizard has a flattened body but no conspicuous pointed horns.

Distribution:

Southwestern United States from southeastern Oregon and southwestern Idaho to southeastern California and western Arizona and into northern Baja California and extreme northwestern Mexico. The Desert Horned Lizard occurs in non-mountainous parts of Malheur and southern Harney and Lake Counties. It is known to occur up to at least 4,800 feet (1,460 m) at Follyfarm, Harney County.

Habits and Habitat:

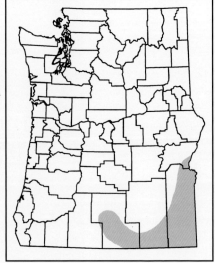

Desert Horned Lizards are usually found in open desert areas where the soil is sandy to gravelly with a sparse to moderate growth of desert shrubs, such as greasewood, saltbush or sagebrush. During the hottest part of the summer, these lizards are usually most active in the early to late morning. They feed heavily on ants and to a lesser extent on beetles, only occasionally taking other insects. They can often be found waiting beside an ant trail, picking up ants as they appear.

When approached by a human, the Desert Horned Lizard is likely to

Adult (Harney County, Oregon)
Photo by William P. Leonard

Adult (Harney County, Oregon)
Photo by William P. Leonard

remain motionless, relying on its protective color to be undetected. If forced to move, the lizard will run under the nearest shrub and remain under its protective cover until it seems safe to emerge. When picked up, this lizard often attempts to press its horns into ones hand.

Desert Horned Lizards show a wide range of body temperatures while active, and can be referred to as relaxed thermoregulators. This lessens the time spent warming up to and maintaining a certain temperature so they can spend more time feeding in open areas. They hibernate in the loose soil among the roots of desert shrubs, usually emerging in April. Nine to thirteen eggs are buried in sandy soil in late May or June, hatching in around two months, in August. The newly hatched young are about 1.6 inches (40 mm) in total length.

Remarks:

There are two subspecies of the Desert Horned Lizard, but only the Northern Desert Horned Lizard, *Phrynosoma platyrhinos platyrhinos* occurs in our area. Desert Horned Lizards are fairly easy to capture and are often taken home as pets. Unfortunately, they invariably die after a few weeks and should not be removed from the desert.

Adult (Owyhee County, Idaho)

Photo by William P. Leonard

Underside of an adult male showing femoral pores (Harney County, Oregon)

Photo by William P. Leonard

Adult (Harney County, Oregon)

Photo by William P. Leonard

SAGEBRUSH LIZARD
Sceloporus graciosus Baird and Girard

Description:

T his small lizard **appears gray or brown** when first seen. Closer examination reveals a usual pattern of a **narrow light gray dorsal stripe running from the head onto the tail.** This is **adjoined on each side by a darker gray or brown stripe, and each of these is bordered below by a light gray stripe, the entire arrangement giving a striped appearance.** The dorsal scales are small but not granular, having a free posterior edge. Ventrally, **males possess blue to blue-black patches on each side of the abdomen and a mottled blue throat, the latter being quite light in some. Females lack the abdominal patches, but may show faint gray to bluish markings at the lateral edges of the abdomen. The female's throat is plain to lightly mottled.** Females develop an orange coloration on the sides of the head and body during the spring breeding season. Sagebrush Lizards reach at least 2.4 inches (62 mm) in snout-vent length and 5.9 inches (150 mm) in total length. Males attain a slightly larger size than females.

Similar Species:

Western Fence Lizards adults are considerably larger, have a double or single solid blue throat patch, keeled scales on the backs of the thighs, yellow on the backs of the hind limbs, and larger more pointed dorsal scales. Side-blotched Lizards have granular non-pointed scales and a gular skin fold on the forepart of the chest.

Distribution:

Western United States from eastern Washington, southern Idaho, southern Montana and extreme western North Dakota to northwestern New Mexico and northern Baja California. Isolated populations in eastern New Mexico and western Texas. Widely scattered in eastern Washington, except absent from the northeastern part. It ranges in Washington up to about 1,618 feet (493 m) near Coulee City, Grant County. In Oregon, occurs in the vicinity of the Columbia River east of the Cascades, then from a line between southern Jefferson County and southern Baker County southward to the Oregon

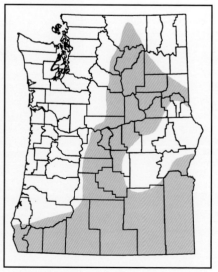

Adult (Saddle Mountain National Wildlife Refuge, Washington)
Photo by William R. Radke

Adult (Harney County, Oregon)
Photo by William P. Leonard

border. Also occurs in the Rogue River drainage of southwestern Oregon. Known to occur to at least 5,000 feet (1,524 m) in elevation on the lower western slopes of Steens Mountain.

Habits and Habitat:

As their names implies, Sagebrush Lizards inhabit a large part of the sagebrush plains of eastern Washington and Oregon. However, they may also occur in extensive stands of greasewood or other desert shrubs. They can be found in open juniper or pine woodlands where there is brushy cover beneath the trees. If the larger Western Fence Lizard is absent from rocky areas, Sagebrush Lizards may occur there. The two species seldom occur together, but in a juniper woodland in Deschutes County, Oregon, Western Fence Lizards occur on large rock outcrops while Sagebrush Lizards use small outcrops and shrubs in the vicinity.

Sagebrush Lizards usually emerge from hibernation in April and even on cool days may be seen basking in sunny openings, often perched on small rocks. Mating occurs in April and May and females deposit two to seven eggs in June, burying them in loose soil at the base of a shrub. Hatching normally occurs in August, the hatchlings being about an inch (25 mm) in snout-vent length.

Sagebrush Lizards are extremely wary during basking and activity periods, dashing quickly into cover beneath shrubs when approached. They feed by stalking a variety of insects and other small invertebrates. They are probably preyed upon by some snakes (e.g., Racers and Striped Whipsnakes) and avian predators.

Remarks:

Depending on the source, three or four subspecies of *Sceloporus graciosus* are recognized. Of the three subspecies, only the Northern Sagebrush Lizard (*Sceloporus graciosus graciosus*) occurs in our area. A possible fourth subspecies, the Southern Sagebrush Lizard (*Sceloporus graciosus gracilis*) occupies extreme southwestern Oregon, to the exclusion of the Northern Sagebrush Lizard.

Underside of an adult female (Harney County, Oregon)
Photo by William P. Leonard

Underside of an adult male (Harney County, Oregon)
Photo by William P. Leonard

WESTERN FENCE LIZARD
Sceloporus occidentalis Baird and Girard

Description:

T his common moderately large lizard is **usually some shade of gray or brown to almost black. The large dorsal scales are keeled and conspicuously free and pointed at the posterior ends.** In lighter-colored individuals, **there may be a pattern of wavy dark and light bands across the back, or a row of chevron-like (V-shaped) or triangular blotches down each side of the back.** These become obscure or less evident in near-black individuals. Male Western Fence Lizards often show a liberal sprinkling of blue-green (turquoise) flecks on the back and upper tail base. **Ventrally, there are large blue patches on each side of the abdomen and a somewhat divided or solid blue patch on the throat.** These colors are lighter in females. In males, the space between the blue abdominal patches and below the throat (gular) may be more or less heavily suffused with black. The posterior surfaces of the hind limbs are yellow to orange, and the scales there are keeled.

Western Fence Lizards living in Washington and western Oregon range up to 3.2 inches (81 mm) in snout-vent length and 6.6 inches (168 mm) in total length. In eastern Oregon, they may attain 3.9 inches (99 mm) in snout-vent length and 8.4 inches (213 mm) in total length. (See below under Remarks.)

Similar Species:

Sagebrush Lizards are smaller as adults, have smaller scales, lack the solid blue throat patch, do not have yellow on the backs of the hind limbs and do not have keeled scales on the backs of the thighs.

Distribution:

Central Washington south through Oregon, southwest Idaho and western Utah to northern Baja California. In Washington, Western Fence Lizards occur in scattered localities around Puget Sound, in the Columbia Gorge and along the east flank of the Cascades. There are also a few records in the Blue Mountains in extreme southeastern Washington. They range through western Oregon except for coastal areas north of Coos County, and are widespread east of the Cascades in Oregon, except for the north-central part. They occur up to at least 5,000

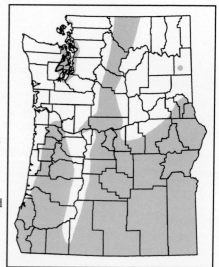

Adult (Klickitat County, Washington)
Photo by William P. Leonard

Adult (Harney County, Oregon)
Photo by William P. Leonard

feet (1,524 m) in southeastern Oregon, and to 3,717 feet (1,134 m) in Manashtash Canyon in Kittitas County, Washington.

Habits and Habitat:

Western Fence Lizards avoid flat valley floors and humid forests. In areas west of the Cascades, they occur in foothill areas, logged-off areas, clearings and open second-growth. They require elevated perches and utilize stumps, logs, rocks, old buildings, wooden fences, etc. In eastern parts of their distribution, they inhabit rocky rims, canyons and boulder-strewn hillsides. They are adept climbers on tree trunks and rocky surfaces.

Depending on where they occur, Western Fence Lizards emerge from hibernation from early March through April, the males usually coming out ahead of the females. The males are territorial and utilize elevated perches to display by doing pushups while puffing out the throat and contracting the sides to better show their blue patches. Egg-laying occurs from late May into early July, the clutch of a usual eight or nine eggs being buried in somewhat moist loose soil or placed in a cavity in a log or under a rock. Hatching occurs about two months later in August or September.

Western Fence Lizards can be approached fairly closely if one is careful, and can be observed as they go about their routines of displaying, courting, mating and feeding. They feed mainly on insects, but also take other small invertebrates. If approached too closely, a lizard often moves to the other side of its perch, showing only its head to the watcher.

Remarks:

Two subspecies of the Western Fence Lizard, from a total of six, occur in our area. The Northwestern Fence Lizard (*Sceloporus occidentalis occidentalis*) occurs throughout the Washington range of the species (except for extreme southeastern Washington). In Oregon, it occurs in western Oregon and probably in the Deschutes River Valley east of the Cascades. This subspecies is smaller (to 6.6 inches in total length) and has a somewhat divided throat patch. The Great Basin Fence Lizard (*Sceloporus occidentalis longipes*) occurs in extreme southeastern Washington and throughout the remainder of eastern Oregon. It is larger (to 8.4 inches in total length) and the blue throat patch is solid.

Adult male
(Shasta County,
California)

Photo by William P. Leonard

Underside of a male
(Deschutes County,
Oregon)

Photo by William P. Leonard

Adult (Deschutes
County, Oregon)

Photo by William P. Leonard

SIDE-BLOTCHED LIZARD
Uta stansburiana Baird and Girard

Description:

Side-blotched Lizards are the **smallest** lizards in our area. They **appear gray to brown** from a little distance, but show further characteristics when close. **Both sexes have tiny rounded (granular) back scales, a blue-black spot behind each front leg and a transverse skin fold (gular fold) across the front part of the chest. Males are slightly larger than females and usually show a liberal sprinkling of light blue (turquoise) spots on the back. Males may also have an orange suffusion on the chin, sides of the body and underside of the tail.** Females lack the dorsal blue flecks or show them only slightly and they may have a slight orange suffusion on the sides. Female backs are sprinkled with dark flecks, and a line of rather V-shaped spots runs down the top surface of the tail. Adults are up to a little over 2 inches (54 mm) in snout-vent length and to about 5 inches (130 mm) in total length.

Similar Species:

Sagebrush and Western Fence Lizards have larger pointed scales and lack a gular fold. Side-blotched lizards are probably smaller than hatchlings of the following three species, and can be further separated by the characteristic given for each: Desert Collared Lizard- two black collars; Long-nosed Leopard Lizard- light dorsal crossbands; Western Whiptail Lizard- large squared ventral scales.

Distribution:

South-central Washington, southwestern Idaho and Utah to southern California, Baja California, New Mexico and western Texas. Extends north in central Washington to southern Douglas County. Widespread in eastern Oregon, except absent from about the northeastern quarter of that area. Known to occur up to 5,900 feet (1,800 m) in elevation in Oregon and up to 1,712 feet (522 m) near Vantage, Grant County, Washington.

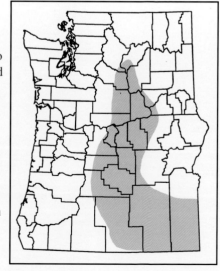

Habits and Habitat:

Side-blotched Lizards are known to inhabit a variety of habitats, including desert flats, having sandy and gravelly soil and at least some shrubs,

Adult male (Harney County, Oregon)
Photo by William P. Leonard

Adult (Saddle Mountain National Wildlife Refuge, Washington)
Photo by William R. Radke

to rocky rims and canyon walls. They tend to avoid areas with trees, but are quite adept at climbing over rocky surfaces, even when these are quite steep.

On any given spring or summer day, Side-blotched Lizards are usually the first to become active, probably being able to warm up more quickly because of their small size. As the weather becomes hotter, these lizards are active during the morning, take an afternoon siesta and emerge again during the last half of the afternoon. They feed on insects and other small arthropods, usually stalking these when they spot them.

Side-blotched Lizards emerge from hibernation in late March and are soon courting and mating. The males, at least, are territorial and display their colors by head-bobbing and push-ups, at which time they can be approached quite closely. Females may produce two clutches of two to five eggs each per year, laying the first in late April or May. The eggs are usually buried in loose soil and hatch in about two months.

In areas where they occur, Side-blotched Lizards are likely to be the most abundant lizard species. Because they often carry on their usual activities in the near presence of a human watcher, one can spend many pleasant minutes observing them.

Remarks:

There are five subspecies of the Side-blotched Lizard, but only the Northern Side-blotched Lizard (*Uta stansburiana stansburiana*) occurs in the Northwest.

Adult female (Harney County, Oregon)

Photo by William P. Leonard

Underside of an adult exposing the gular fold (Harney County, Oregon)

Photo by William P. Leonard

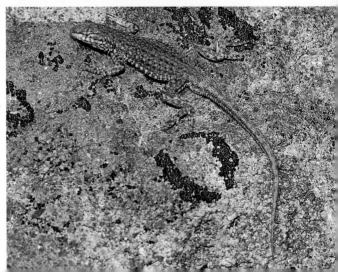

Adult female (Harney County, Oregon)

Photo by William P. Leonard

WESTERN SKINK
Eumeces skiltonianus (Baird and Girard)

Description:

A small to medium-sized lizard with **smooth shiny scales** arranged much like rounded roof shingles. **A wide brown dorsal stripe is bordered on each side by a contrasting lighter stripe,** each of which is bordered below by a dark brown to black stripe. All stripes begin on the head and extend onto the tail base. The **tail is bright blue in young animals,** becoming more blue-gray to brownish with age. During the breeding season, adult males develop an orange suffusion on the chin and sides of the head. Snout-vent length is up to 3 inches (76 mm), total length to 7.9 inches (201 mm).

Similar Species:

No other lizard in our area is covered with fairly uniform smooth shiny scales arranged in contrasting longitudinal stripes. Young Western Whiptails (*Cnemidophorus tigris*) have a light blue tail, but have tiny granular scales dorsally and large squared scales ventrally.

Distribution:

South-central British Columbia through Washington, Oregon and Idaho to western Utah, Nevada and southern California and into Baja California. Absent from southeastern California. In Washington, occurs in scattered localities east of the Cascades and in the Columbia Gorge. Widespread in Oregon, but absent from coastal areas north of Curry County, the high Cascades and probably the far southeastern area. They have been found in Washington at elevations ranging between 400 feet (121 m) near Lyle and 3,257 feet (993 m) north of Chelan, Chelan County.

Habits and Habitat:

Western Skinks are found on grassy slopes in oak woodlands and in less damp coniferous forests in western Oregon. East of the Cascades, in both states, they occur in pine and juniper woodlands, rocky canyons, and rimrock areas. In wooded areas, they may be found within or under the bark of decaying logs or under surface debris or rocks. In more treeless areas, they usually occur in loose rock accumulations such as small talus runs. They occur to at least 5000 feet (1,524 m) on

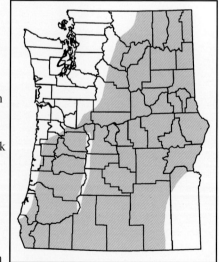

Adult (Klickitat County, Washington)
Photo by William P. Leonard

Adult (Columbia National Wildlife Refug, Washington)
Photo by William R. Radke

the slopes of Steens Mountain in southeastern Oregon.

At a site in western Klickitat County, one of us (Leonard) found three individuals apparently denning with Northern Alligator Lizards, Rubber Boas, and both Northwestern and Common Garter Snakes. All were found together among and beneath rocks on a south-facing rock outcrop.

Western Skinks are usually diurnal foragers, moving with rather jerky motions within their habitat. One may often hear the rustling of grass or leaves as they move through them, feeding on a variety of small invertebrates.

They are capable of burrowing for short distances. If one attempts to capture a skink, the blue tail often breaks off and continues to wiggle for several minutes, probably drawing a predator's attention away from the escaping Skink.

Little is known of the life history of this species in the Northwest. They are thought to mate in May or June, and two to six eggs are laid in flask-shaped burrows under rocks or logs in June or July. Females remain with the eggs, not only attempting to guard them, but possibly occasionally basking in the sun and then returning to the eggs, thus bringing additional heat to them. Hatching occurs in late July or August, the female staying with the young briefly, prior to their dispersal.

Remarks:

There are four subspecies of the Western Skink, only two of which may occur in our area. *Eumeces skiltonianus skiltonianus*, the Skilton Skink, occurs throughout as explained under Distribution. *Eumeces skiltonianus utahensis*, the Great Basin Skink, may occur in extreme southeastern Malheur County, Oregon. The two subspecies can be separated on the basis of their longitudinal stripes.

Adult male (Jackson County, Oregon)
Photo by William P. Leonard

Hatchling (Columbia National Wildlife Refuge, Washington)
Photo by William R. Radke

WESTERN WHIPTAIL
Cnemidophorus tigris Baird and Girard

Description:

T his long-tailed desert lizard appears dark gray to brown at a distance but shows a more complex coloration when close-up. The back area behind the head **appears to consist of four gray to brown longitudinal stripes separated by very irregular (crooked) black lines and blotches.** The sides of the body are marked with dark blotches that often seem to form roughly vertical lines. The tail is a rather uniform gray-brown. The **scales of the back and sides are tiny and granular. Ventrally, the large squared scales (eight rows) are increasingly marked with black as one goes from tail to head.** The snout tends to be pointed or cone-shaped and the head joins the body with no obvious neck. The snout-vent length is up to 4.5 inches (112 mm) and total length reaches at least 13 inches (330 mm). In juveniles, the longitudinal stripes are more evident and the tail is gray-blue.

Similar Species:

No other lizard in our area displays the combination of granular dorsal scales and large square ventral scales, with the exception of the introduced Plateau Striped Whiptail (*Cnemidophorus velox*), which occurs in a small area adjacent to Lake Billy Chinook, outside the Oregon range of the Western Whiptail. Blue-tailed juveniles may resemble young Western Skinks, but the latter have much bluer tails and their dorsal scales are larger and shiny smooth.

Distribution:

From southeastern Oregon and southwestern Idaho through the southwestern United States into Baja California and northern Mexico. In our area, in the extreme southeastern corner of Oregon in southeastern Baker County, Malheur County and eastern Harney County. Disjunct populations occur in the John Day Fossil Beds National Monument and in the Diamond Craters area. They range in elevation from 2,400 feet (732 m) in the John Day Fossil Beds to over 5,000 feet (1,524 m) on Pueblo Mountain, Harney County, Oregon.

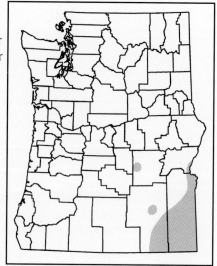

Adult (Harney County, Oregon)
Photo by William P. Leonard

Adult (Harney County, Oregon)
Photo by William P. Leonard

Habits and Habitat:

These lizards inhabit the brushy desert regions of southeastern Oregon. They are most likely to occur in areas of firm sandy or silty soil with a good growth of shrubs such as greasewood, saltbush or sagebrush. During the summer, they are most active in the early to mid-morning period when they can be seen foraging on the ground between shrubs. They move with short dashes and quick stops, frequently flicking their tongues against the substrate or pushing their noses into the soil. They may occasionally dig with front feet to procure a buried insect larva, which they probably detect by odor. They feed mostly on insect larvae and adults, but are known to take an occasional small lizard.

When approached by a person, these lizards often run to a nearby shrub and then quietly move under its shelter to sneak away on the other side. At other times, they have been seen to run 100 meters or more to enter a burrow, indicating a known home range.

The Western Whiptail usually emerges from hibernation in late April or early May. Mating probably occurs in May or early June, followed by egg-laying in late June or early July. One to four eggs, measuring 0.4 by 0.7 inches (10 by 17 mm) are placed underground where they hatch sometime in August. Females in our area produce only one clutch per year. In most years, these lizards may become inactive (aestivate) during the hottest part of the summer (late July and August), resurfacing for a few weeks in late August or early September before entering hibernation in late September.

Remarks:

There are six subspecies of the Western Whiptail in the United States, but only the Great Basin Whiptail, *Cnemidophorus tigris tigris*, occurs in our area. Western Whiptails have been know to emit a "squeek" when captured and held in the hand.

Underside of an adult (Harney County, Oregon)
Photo by William P. Leonard

Juvenile (Idaho)
Photo by Charles R. Peterson

PLATEAU STRIPED WHIPTAIL

Cnemidophorus velox Springer   {Introduced}

Description:

This is an **obviously striped lizard with a light blue tail (brighter blue in juveniles). There are six or seven dorsal light stripes, separated by dark brown wider stripes.** Like other whiptails, the **dorsal scales are granular, while the ventrals are large and squarish. The throat and belly are white,** often with a bluish-green tinge. Snout vent length is 2.5 to 3.5 inches (62-89 mm) and total length is 8 to 10.7 inches (203-272 mm).

Similar Species:

Western Skink has enlarged dorsal scales; Western Whiptail shows heavy invasion of black on chest scales and the dorsal pattern is not one of clean-edged stripes.

Distribution:

The Plateau Striped Whiptail is native to the Four Corners area, where Utah, Colorado, Arizona and New Mexico join. It was introduced to central Oregon sometime prior to 1970, and since then has occurred in Cove Palisades State Park, Jefferson County, where it inhabits rocky juniper-grown areas adjacent to an outdoor storage place for discarded park equipment. This is on the west side of Lake Billy Chinook.

Habitats and Habitat:

Prefers open woodland areas with a grassy understory in its original southwestern distribution. In Oregon, it is fairly common in juniper woodlands with scant ground vegetation and gravelly soil adjacent to a large paved parking lot. Feeds on insects. Said to lay three to five eggs, which hatch without male fertilization. All individuals are females (parthenogenetic).

Remarks:

It is probable that only a single female was needed to be transported to Oregon to start this population. The Plateau Striped Whiptail offers a fine opportunity for a study of its present distribution and its ecology and life history in Oregon.

Adult female (Jefferson County, Oregon)

Photo by Robert M. Storm

Adult female (Jefferson County, Oregon)

Photo by Robert M. Storm

Adult female (San Juan County, New Mexico)

Photo by John S. Applegarth

RUBBER BOA
Charina bottae (Blainville)

Description:

R ubber Boas receive their name from the **rubbery feel and appearance of their skin.** Rubber Boas are **uniform in color dorsally, varying from olive green to light or dark brown. The young may be tan or pink.** Lilac colored individuals have been found in western Oregon. Rubber Boas are small to medium-sized snakes, **usually less than two feet (600 mm) long** with a maximum length of 33 inches (830 mm). They are stout-bodied, with a **small, wedge-shaped head, and an indistinct neck.** The top of the head is covered with large plates. Their **eyes are small with vertical pupils.** The **lack of enlarged chin shields** is a distinctive feature from other snakes in our area. Their **dorsal scales are small and smooth.** Rubber Boas **have a short, blunt tail that resembles the head;** consequently, they are sometimes called two-headed snakes. The terminal tail vertebrae are fused into a hard, bony cone underlying the skin. Rubber Boas possess vestiges of hind limbs called **anal spurs,** which are located beside the cloaca. The spurs of the males are larger and hooked downward, but those of females are smaller, project straight to rear, and may not be visible. Females reach greater lengths and weights than do males, but have relatively shorter tails.

Similar Species:

The distinctive characteristics of Rubber Boas make it unlikely that they will be confused with other species of snakes in Washington or Oregon. Racers might be confused with Rubber Boas because of their smooth scales and uniform dorsal coloration. However, Racers are longer and thinner, have large eyes with round pupils, possess a long, pointed tail, and crawl much faster than boas.

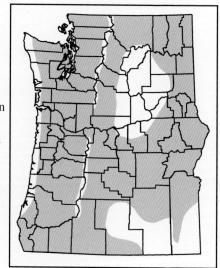

Distribution:

Rubber Boas range from southern British Columbia to the mountains of southern California and east to western Montana and Wyoming. They occur throughout most of Washington and Oregon, except for most of the coastal areas and some sagebrush areas in central Washington and Oregon. Within this range, they are spottily distributed, and occur up to 4,236 feet (1,292 m) near Clearwater Guard

94

Adult (Siskiyou County, California)
Photo by William P. Leonard

Adult (Klickitat County, Washington)
Photo by William P. Leonard

Station in the Blue Mountains, Garfield County, Washington and to 6,200 feet (1,890 m) on Hart Mountain, Lake County, Oregon.

Habits and Habitat:

Rubber Boas are found in a wide variety of habitats, ranging from deserts and grasslands to woodlands and mountain forests. They usually occur within several hundred yards (meters) of water. Microhabitats include rotting stumps or logs, bark, flat rocks, crevices in cliffs, and forest litter (leaves, pine needles, etc.). Rubber Boas are semifossorial but also can climb and swim well. They are secretive and primarily move around at night to forage or disperse. However, Rubber Boas (especially pregnant females) will bask. Because of their fossorial and nocturnal habits, Rubber Boas usually are difficult to observe. Although they may appear to be uncommon or rare, under the appropriate conditions they can be common to abundant.

Rubber Boas hibernate in the winter and are usually active from March through November. Breeding occurs during April and May. In cooler areas, the activity season will be shorter and females will not reproduce every year. Rubber Boas are very cold tolerant; active individuals have been measured with body temperatures less than 44° F (7° C). Pregnant females may congregate in areas that allow them to maintain warm, stable body temperatures. Two to eight young are born in the late summer or fall (August to November). Rubber boas can live a long time; for example, a female, collected as an adult in 1977, is still in captivity after 18 years.

Rubber boas feed primarily on small rodents and shrews but have been reported to also eat salamanders, lizards, snakes, and birds. They will raid rodent nests and are reported to fend off the mother with their tails while swallowing the young rodents. Like other true boas, they kill their prey by constricting (suffocating) it.

By moving slowly and being active at night, Rubber Boas are probably able to avoid detection by many predators. If threatened while they are near a burrow or crevice, Rubber Boas will generally seek to escape. In some other situations, they will coil into a ball and hide their head underneath their body. To divert an attack away from the head, they will wave their tail in the air and even strike with it. They also will emit a strong musk which may serve to deter potential predators such as skunks and owls.

Remarks:

In the past, two to three subspecies were distinguished on the basis of scalation differences. However, no subspecies of Rubber Boas are currently recognized.

Juvenile (Kittitas County, Washington)
Photo by William P. Leonard

Adult (Siskiyou County, California)
Photo by John S. Applegarth

RACER
Coluber constrictor   Linnaeus

Description:

T he Racers of Washington and Oregon are of a **uniform olive to bluish gray dorsally with a yellowish venter which often becomes more white toward the throat and head.** The ventral coloration varies in its intensity throughout the region with western Oregon populations tending toward a more whitish or cream color. The visual acuity of the Racer is reflected in its relatively **large eyes.** Scales are smooth and occur in rows of 15-17 on the midbody. Adult total lengths range from 20 to 48 inches (50-120 cm). Hatchlings have been recorded with total lengths of approximately 8.5 inches (215-220 mm). The color pattern of hatchlings and juveniles is distinctly different from that of adults. Young snakes exhibit brownish saddle-shaped blotches which grade into a uniform tail color much like adult snakes. As snakes age, the blotches disappear from the tail forward, gradually giving way to the uniform coloration of the adult.

Similar Species:

Young Racers might be mistaken for young Gopher Snakes but have smooth scales, larger eyes, and uniform coloration toward the tail. Night Snakes are also similar to young Racers but have vertical pupils.

Distribution:

Racers range widely in North America from southern Canada to Guatemala. They are found in the Pacific Northwest as far north as southern British Columbia. While this species is found throughout Oregon, in Washington it is found primarily east of the Cascades and in the Columbia Gorge. Racers have not been found in western Washington since 1939 and now appear to be extirpated there.

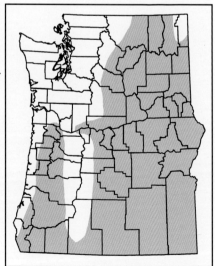

The Racer ranges in elevation between 200 feet (61 m) along the Columbia River in Klickitat County, Washington and Wasco County, Oregon, up to 3,542 feet (1,080 m) north of Chelan, Chelan County, Washington, and to 5,600 feet (1,707 m) on Hart Mountain, Lake County, Oregon.

Adult (Kittitas County, Washington)
Photo by William P. Leonard

Adult (Columbia National Wildlife Refuge, Washington)
Photo by William R. Radke

Habits and Habitats:

These diurnal snakes are most often found in various types of open habitat such as meadows, sagebrush flats, and talus slopes. They can live in moist to semi-arid areas, but are seldom found in forests. They are primarily ground dwellers but will climb in the lower branches of shrubs. In the Pacific Northwest, Racers emerge from their dens in April or May and are active during the warmest part of the day. Mating takes place after emergence from the den, usually in May. Clutches of 3-7 eggs are laid in late June or early July, sometimes in aggregations with other snakes and lizards. Eggs are rounded (approximately 35 mm long and 20 mm wide) and have a granular texture. Hatching takes place approximately 50 days after laying in mid- to late-August. As their name implies, Racers are fast and sometimes difficult to catch. When they are captured, they often exhibit aggression toward the captor. They are sometimes seen cruising through grassland with the head held above the vegetation using their visual acuity to search for prey. Racers are known to den with various other species of snake - Western Rattlesnake, Striped Whipsnake, Gopher Snake, Night Snake, Rubber Boa, Ringneck Snake, Longnose Snake, and Garter Snakes. Upon emergence from the den, dispersal distance may be as far as 1.8 km with typical distances being less than half of that. Most Racers return to the same den site each fall and to the same home range each summer. The method of orientation is not well understood, but olfactory cues are suspected. Adult Racers feed on small mammals, lizards, frogs and, insects. Young feed primarily on insects, especially grasshoppers and crickets. In spite of the scientific name of this species, feeding is not by constriction, although loops of the body are used to immobilize the prey.

Remarks:

Currently ten subspecies of the Racer are recognized in the United States. Only one, the Western Yellowbelly Racer, *Coluber constrictor mormon*, is found in Washington and Oregon. This is the only widespread U. S. subspecies found west of the Rocky Mountains, and some herpetologists have suggested that it should be recognized as a separate species, *Coluber mormon*.

Adult (Jackson County, Oregon)

Photo by William P. Leonard

Underside of an adult exposing yellow ventrals (Jackson County, Oregon)

Photo by William P. Leonard

Juvenile (Benton County, Oregon)

Photo by Robert M. Storm

SHARPTAIL SNAKE
Contia tenuis (Baird and Girard)

Description:

T he Sharptail Snake receives its name because of the **spine-like tip of its tail**. Dorsal coloration is reddish-brown to gray with the reddish intensifying towards the tail. The head is usually dark brown above. **Narrow dorsolateral red stripes extend to the tip of the tail** and mark the border of the dorsal coloration and the lateral gray of the head and body. **Distinct ventral crossbars of black and white or cream** are present anterior to the vent. Scales are smooth with the most posterior modified into the spine-like tail tip. Sharptail Snakes are relatively small, averaging approximately 12 inches (30 cm) in total length and ranging from 8 to 16 inches (20-40 cm). Young are reddish above with fine dark lines on the sides and range in total length from 3.5 to 4 inches (89-104 mm).

Similar Species:

Rarely, melanistic Ringneck Snakes have been reported without the characteristic neck ring and with a pattern of ventral crossbars similar to the Sharptail Snake. However, these melanistic Ringneck Snakes are darker dorsally and lack the tail spine.

Distribution:

Sharptail Snakes range from British Columbia to central coastal California and into the southern extent of the Sierra Nevada. In Washington and Oregon, distribution is spotty, but these snakes may be locally common. Populations are usually restricted to lower elevations and are found primarily on the west side of the Cascades from southern Oregon to the Puget Sound area. Populations on the east side of the Cascades occur from northern Oregon (Wasco County) to central Washington (Chelan County). British Columbia populations are restricted to Vancouver Island and neighboring islands. They range in elevation from near sea-level up to 2,000 feet (610 m) near Cle Elum, Kittitas County, Washington, and to similar elevations in Oregon.

Habits and Habitats:

These secretive snakes occur in damp conditions at lower temperatures

Adult (Kittitas County, Washington)
Photo by William P. Leonard

Underside of an adult exposing banded ventrals (Kittitas County, Washington)
Photo by William P. Leonard

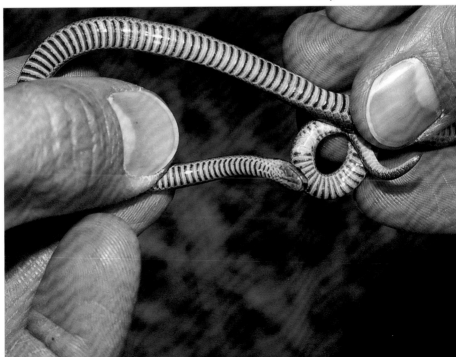

(10° - 17° C) than most other species of snake. They are often found after rainy periods under cover or in talus at forest edges or in open meadows. Open water is often nearby. If conditions are favorable, individuals tend to aggregate. In the Willamette Valley, the period of activity is from late February through November with peak activity from late March through early June. A second period of higher activity occurs from late September through November. Eggs are deposited in June or July and hatch in the fall. Each female lays 3 to 5 eggs; however, clutches of up to 9 eggs have been found indicating communal nesting behavior. Sharptail Snakes feed almost exclusively on slugs. This restrictive diet is reflected morphologically by the presence of unusually long teeth which are presumably an adaptation for capturing, subduing, and manipulating such prey. The distribution and activity patterns are apparently correlated to diet as well. Sharptails are found only in places and at times when slugs are present. When captured, individuals usually thrash about and may press the tail spine against the captor's skin in such a way as to suggest its function as an anti predator device. It has also been proposed as an aid in burrowing. Its adaptive role, if any, remains a mystery.

Remarks:

The Sharptail Snake was originally described as a species in 1852 based on a specimen collected in the "Puget Sound Region" but was not "rediscovered" in Washington until 1939 when a specimen was found in the basement of a house by Gravelly Lake near Tacoma, Washington. Very few sightings of Sharptail Snakes have been reported from the Puget Sound Region since 1939.

The most common small slugs found within the range of Sharptail Snakes, and likely the most common prey item, are members of a genus of slug introduced from Europe. Native species of slugs of proper size for feeding are far less common. It is not known which native species of slug may have previously been the primary prey item for Sharptail Snakes, but the introduction of the European slugs has undoubtedly modified the ecological distribution of these snakes.

The relationship of Sharptail Snakes to other snake species is unclear, and current thought shows them to stand quite alone evolutionarily.

Adult (Kittitas County, Washington)

Photo by William P. Leonard

Adult (Jackson County, Oregon)

Photo by William P. Leonard

Adult (Jackson County, Oregon)

Photo by William P. Leonard

RINGNECK SNAKE
Diadophis punctatus (Linnaeus)

Description:

The Ringneck Snake is named because of the usually **distinct bright orange-red neck band 1-1/2 to 2-1/2 scales wide.** The **ventral surface is also bright orange-red,** grading into a more pure red on the underside of the tail. Dorsal coloration is a dark slate green becoming darker on the head. The **belly is flecked with black** with the flecks becoming more numerous on the throat and chin. Scales are smooth, although in males the scales just above the vent have ridges. These snakes range in total length from 8 to 30 inches (20-75 cm), with few specimens in the Pacific Northwest reaching 20 inches (50 cm). Females are larger than males. Hatchlings have been recorded with total lengths of 7 to 8 inches (174-208 mm). Young are very dark, almost black, dorsally.

Similar Species:

No other snake in the Pacific Northwest exhibits the bright orange-red neck band and ventral coloration of the Ringneck Snake.

Distribution:

Ringneck Snakes range widely in the eastern and midwestern United States but are more restricted in the west. In Oregon, this species is found primarily west of the Cascades while in Washington it is found in the Columbia River Gorge, in the south-central portion of the state just east of the Cascades (as far north as Kittitas County), and in the southeastern corner of the state. Ringneck Snakes occur from near sea level along the Columbia River in Cowlitz County to 2461 feet (750 m) along Manashtash Creek, Kittitas County, Washington. Distribution in Oregon is largely below 2,500 feet (762 m) in elevation.

Habits and Habitats:

These snakes are usually found in moist conditions under wood, rocks, talus, boards, or debris. Although often found in wooded areas, they also occur in open habitats. In the Pacific Northwest, Ringneck Snakes are active from March through November and are most active at temperatures ranging from 21°-31° C.

Females reproduce annually after attaining sexual maturity in their third

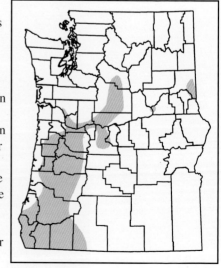

Adult (Jackson County, Oregon)
Photo by Robert M. Storm

Adult (Jackson County, Oregon)
Photo by William P. Leonard

spring and lay eggs in early July in talus or rotting logs. Clutch size ranges from 1-10 with 3 or 4 eggs per female being common. Eggs are elongate (approximately 25 mm long and 10 mm wide). These snakes are sometimes highly gregarious, with some populations showing high densities. Individuals can be long-lived (15 years) and often return to the same den site.

Although diet differs geographically, Ringneck Snakes feed primarily on salamanders and lizards when available, but also take frogs, smaller snakes, insects, slugs, and earthworms. Feeding may be aided by toxic salivary secretions. Enlarged rear teeth on the upper jaw, chewing behavior during feeding, and excessive salivation upon capture are all indicative of a venomous snake. In addition, when alarmed, these snakes will tightly coil the tail and expose the bright red ventral surface, suggesting aposematic coloration. The saliva appears to paralyze prey items but is apparently not harmful to humans.

Remarks:

Most sources currently recognize twelve subspecies of the Ringneck Snake in the United States. Six of these occur in the Pacific States with only the Northwestern Ringneck Snake, *Diadophis punctatus occidentalis*, occurring in Washington and Oregon. One recent proposal suggests that this subspecies should actually be classified as *Diadophis amabolis occidentalis*.

Adult (Skamania County, Washington)
Photo by William P. Leonard

Adult (Klickitat County, Washington)
Photo by Kate Slavens

NIGHT SNAKE
Hypsiglena torquata (Gunther)

Description:

The Night Snake is a small snake which seldom exceeds 24 inches (61 cm) in total length. The **dorsal surface is a light tan color with dark tan to brown blotches extending down the middle of the back above smaller lateral dark spots.** There is a **large blotch behind the head on the neck and a dark stripe along the upper jaw.** Close inspection will reveal that the **eye has a vertical pupil,** similar to the Western Rattlesnake. In living Night Snakes, the underside is a striking lustrous white. Night Snakes have enlarged rear teeth that are capable of delivering venom to their prey, but they do not represent any threat to humans.

Similar Species:

A Night Snake superficially resembles a young Racer or a small Gopher Snake. However, it has vertical pupils and dark upper jaw stripes which are not found in either the Racer or the Gopher Snake.

Distribution:

The Night Snake has been found at scattered locations in the more arid low elevations of eastern Washington (up to 2,028 feet or 619 m) and Oregon (below 4,500 feet or 1,372 m). It is probably more widespread than present records would indicate because its secretive habits make it difficult to find.

Habits and Habitat:

The difficulty of finding Night Snakes greatly reduces our understanding of their habitat and life history requirements.

They are found in arid low-elevation regions, most commonly associated with rocky areas. Work done in southwest Idaho indicates that they are most abundant in rocky areas, but that they can also be found using rodent burrows in areas with low desert shrubs and sandy soils. As the name implies, the snake is most active at night but probably is occasionally active during late evening and early morning hours. Red-tailed Hawks which are only active by day occasionally capture Night Snakes. Night Snakes probably first become active in

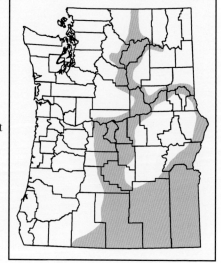

Adult showing vertical pupil (Malheur County, Oregon)
Photo by Robert M. Storm

Adult (Wheeler County, Oregon)
Photo by Robert M. Storm

April, and through the early spring they can be found near the surface in cool sunny weather by turning rocks. Once daytime temperatures become hot, turning rocks is not effective, but they can be seen on the surface at night. One method is by driving slowly on paved roads during a warm night.

Little is known about the foraging of Night Snakes, but their most common prey consists of small lizards (usually the Side-blotched Lizard). They have also been found to take lizard eggs, small frogs or toads and large insects. The venom associated with their rear teeth is able to immobilize and eventually kill prey animals. Females are larger than males and lay three to nine eggs, probably in June. Mating has not been observed, but based on testes development in the male, probably occurs in the spring.

Remarks:

There are no recognized subspecies of the Night Snake. Although considered rare, work done with drift fences in southwestern Idaho showed that they can be locally abundant. The distributions of the Night Snake and the Side-blotched Lizard overlap closely in our area and the snakes may be dependent on the lizard for food. More research using drift fences will help to better understand this interesting snake.

Juvenile (Oregon)

Photo by William P. Leonard

Adult (Owyhee County, Idaho)

Photo by William P. Leonard

Juvenile (Chelan County, Washington)

Photo by William P. Leonard

COMMON KINGSNAKE
Lampropeltis getula (Linnaeus)

Description:

The **alternating black and white bands** make this snake distinctive from others in the Pacific Northwest. The **snout and sides of the head are white,** although the scales of this region exhibit black edges. The **top of the head and region of the neck are black,** sometimes with white spots, and the alternating band pattern continues back from there. The black bands are widest middorsally and do not show any of the tendency toward brown sometimes seen in California populations. Smooth scales are arranged in rows of 23 at mid-body. Maximum size in the Pacific Northwest is approximately 40 inches (100 cm) total length. Young individuals are patterned similar to adults, and hatchlings have been reported ranging from 10-12 inches (245-290 mm) snout-vent-length.

Similar Species:

No other snake in the Pacific Northwest shows the alternating black and white bands of the Common Kingsnake.

Distribution:

This species is widely distributed throughout the southern two thirds of the United States and into Mexico. In the Pacific states, it is widely distributed in California but only reaches inland valleys in the extreme southwestern corner of Oregon (Douglas, Jackson, and Josephine Counties). Elevational records vary from 780 feet (238 m) to 2,200 feet (671 m). It is not found in Washington.

Habits and Habitats:

Throughout its range, this species inhabits many habitat types. However, in Oregon, it seems to be most closely associated with the moist river valleys of the southwestern part of the state and is usually associated with thick vegetation near streams.

Although little is known about the life history of this snake in the Pacific Northwest, information from other parts of its range indicate that mating takes place from mid-March through early June, clutches of 2-12 eggs are laid usually in July, and hatching occurs after approximately 70 days.

Adult (Jackson County, Oregon)
Photo by William P. Leonard

Adult (Jackson County, Oregon)
Photo by William P. Leonard

Common Kingsnakes are active early in the day and again late in the afternoon, although during hot periods, they are active mostly at night. They are primarily terrestrial but have been found climbing in low vegetation. When disturbed they sometimes respond aggressively, striking and vibrating their tail, but sometimes are more passive, taking a seemingly defensive posture with the head hidden under coils of the body. While not especially fast, when in motion, the banding pattern appears to blend into the substrate background. Long-term data indicate that individuals can maintain small areas (a few hundred yards at greatest diameter) of favorable habitat as permanent residences for a number of years.

Reported food items include lizards, snakes, small mammals, birds, bird and reptile eggs, small turtles, and frogs. Killing is by constriction. Snakes, including rattlesnakes, seem to be the preferred food item and it is not unusual for a Common Kingsnake to take a snake as large as itself. When attacking a snake, the Kingsnake will attempt to constrict the victim at the neck. Kingsnakes are immune to rattlesnake venom; therefore, when a rattlesnake encounters a Kingsnake, it will not attempt to bite, but will attack with loops of its body or move away with its head and neck near the substrate.

Remarks:

Currently, eight subspecies of the Common Kingsnake are recognized in the United States. The subspecies of the western states, including the Oregon populations, is the California Kingsnake, *Lampropeltis getula californiae*.

Adult (Douglas County, Oregon)
Photo by John S. Applegarth

CALIFORNIA MOUNTAIN KINGSNAKE
Lampropeltis zonata (Blainville)

Description:

The distinct red, black, and white bands of this species make it one of the most striking snakes in the Pacific Northwest. The coloration pattern begins with a **black snout** which may sometimes be flecked with red. Following the black snout is a **repeated sequence in which a red band is bordered on either side by first black and then white bands.** The red bands are widest as they approach the ventral surface and are narrower and sometimes incomplete mid dorsally. While the ventral coloration is suggestive of the dorsal pattern, it is much less perfect and more variable. It is not uncommon in the Pacific Northwest for adults to reach a total length of 30 inches (75 cm) but large individuals may reach 40 inches (100 cm). Scales are smooth with 23 rows at mid-body.

Similar Species:

While no snake presently known to occur in Washington or Oregon resembles the California Mountain Kingsnake, the Longnose Snake from southwestern Idaho may enter Oregon and is similar in coloration. However, Longnose Snakes have much narrower white bands, more white flecking, a longer snout, and single caudal scales ventrally on the tail. Because of coloration similar to coral snakes, this species has sometimes been referred to as the "Coral King Snake". While the colors are similar, the pattern is quite different. In the Western Coral Snake, the red bands are bordered by white or yellow rather than black. Coral snakes DO NOT occur in Washington or Oregon.

Distribution:

California Mountain Kingsnakes range from southern Washington into Baja California. However, in Washington and Oregon, distribution of this species is quite restricted. It is found in the southwestern corner of Oregon and in western Klamath County. Washington populations occur more than 200 miles north of these Oregon localities and are restricted mostly to the Columbia Gorge in the south-central part of the state (Klickitat and Skamania Counties). Unconfirmed reports from near Sunnyside in Yakima County and from Wasco County, Oregon and the Blue Mountains need to be investigated.

Juvenile (Klickitat County, Washington)
Photo by William P. Leonard

Adult (Jackson County, Oregon)
Photo by John S. Applegarth

Generally found below 300 feet (91 m) in Washington, but known to occur up to about 3,000 feet (914 m) in Oregon.

Habits and Habitats:

Because California Mountain Kingsnakes are rare in the Pacific Northwest, our knowledge of their biology is limited. What we do know is from limited observation in the wild and in captivity. Therefore, any and all observations of this species are valuable. They appear to favor moist habitats of oak and pine forests and chaparral. They are often found under or within rotting logs but may also be found under rocks. While they tend to be diurnal, in hot weather most activity is at night.

Indications are that mating takes place in late May. Females lay 3-8 eggs in June or July with eggs hatching after an incubation period of around 60 days.

Prey consists of lizards, snakes, nestling birds, bird eggs, and small mammals. Prey is killed by constriction, and although there is a superficial resemblance to coral snakes, California Mountain Kingsnake are NOT poisonous.

Remarks:

Because of its coloration, it has been suggested that the California Mountain Kingsnake is a mimic of venomous coral snakes. However, this hypothesis is weakened by the fact that the California Mountain Kingsnake and coral snakes do not presently occur together.

Currently, six subspecies of the California Mountain Kingsnake are recognized. Populations in northern California, Oregon, and Washington supposedly are intermediate between the Saint Helena Mountain Kingsnake, *Lampropeltis zonata zonata*, and the Sierra Mountain Kingsnake, *L. z. multicincta*. This zone of intergradation is as large or larger than the ranges of any of the distinctly recognized subspecies. This situation reflects our poor knowledge of variation in the species in the Pacific Northwest.

Adult (Jackson County, Oregon)
Photo by William P. Leonard

A young Alan D. St. John and friends (Klickitat County, Washington)
Photo by Jim Riggs

STRIPED WHIPSNAKE
Masticophis taeniatus   (Hallowell)

Description:

The Striped Whipsnake is a **long slender fast-moving snake** that can reach a **total length of over five feet (about 1.5 m).** It has relatively large eyes and its scales are smooth. The **back is dark gray to black, the sides cream-colored with solid or dashed black stripes and the belly is cream-colored, changing to pinkish or salmon on the underside of the tail. The sides of the head show a variegated light and dark pattern.**

Similar Species:

The Racer has similar body proportions with a large eye but is uniformly olive or brown above and yellowish on the ventral surface. Some garter snakes have stripes that may somewhat resemble a Striped Whipsnake, but they have rough keeled scales and are not as long and slender.

Distribution:

The Striped Whipsnake occurs in the Columbia Basin in central Washington at elevations up to 1,985 feet (605 m) and in scattered areas in central and southern Oregon at lower elevations (below about 4,800 feet or 1,463 m). It is quite rare throughout most of its range in Washington and Oregon but can be locally abundant in southeastern Oregon.

Habits and Habitat:

The Striped Whipsnake is found in low elevation arid regions with scattered vegetation and open rocky areas. In general, they are most abundant in areas that support a diversity of lizards such as Side-blotched, Long-nosed Leopard, Western Whiptail and Western Fence Lizards. They are known to use communal dens or hibernacula with other snakes such as the Western Rattlesnake and Gopher Snake. They typically first become active in late March or early April with peak activity in May and June.

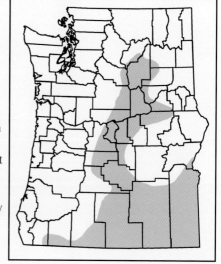

This snake is probably our fastest and most agile snake. It is an active daytime forager that is interesting to observe. When foraging, they typically move along rapidly and then stop and elevate as much as the anterior one-third of their body above the ground.

Adult climbing in shrub
(Saddle Mountain
National Wildlife
Refuge, Washington)

Photo by William R. Radke

Adult climbing in shrub
(Idaho)

Photo by Jon Beck

Adult (Harney County,
Oregon)

Photo by Jon Beck

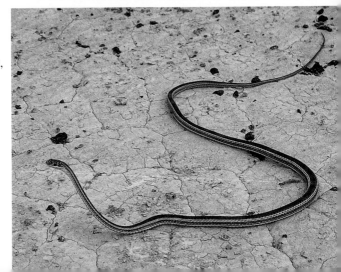

From this position, they will scan the area, looking for the movement of potential prey. If a prey animal is observed, the snake will slowly approach it, attempting to capture it with an initial strike, but if the strike misses, the snake usually pursues the prey. It is a spectacular blur of speed when a Whipsnake pursues a fast-moving lizard like the Western Whiptail. Their most common victims are lizards but they will take a wide variety of prey, including small rodents, bats, frogs, birds and other snakes. They have no specialized mechanism for killing their prey, so they hang on tenaciously and swallow their prey with coordinated movements of their flexible jaws. Because of their speed and agility, Striped Whipsnakes can be difficult to capture by hand. The longitudinal stripes give the illusion that the snake is stationary when it is actually moving. In areas of shrubs and rocks, they can readily outdistance most people. One of us (Diller) has even observed an individual elude him by springing three to four feet from shrub to shrub while he tried to maneuver his way through the shrubs.

Mating occurs in the spring with eggs being deposited in June. Females produce three to ten eggs which hatch in the late summer or early fall. Male combat has been observed in the spring in this species, but the specific context in which this occurs is not known. In one presumed case of male combat that we observed, one large male had grasped another large male by the neck and the two snakes were entwined and thrashing about. One snake received superficial wounds which is inconsistent with the ritualized male combat observed in various species of pit vipers.

Remarks:

Only one subspecies occurs in our area—the Desert Striped Whipsnake, *Masticophis taeniatus taeniatus*.

Underside of an adult exposing salmon color on tail (Idaho)
Photo by Charles R. Peterson

Adult (Harney County, Oregon)
Photo by Robert M. Storm

GOPHER SNAKE
Pituophis catenifer (Blainville)

Description:

The Gopher Snake is one of our largest snakes with adults occasionally getting over four feet (122 cm) in total length. Most adults, however, are between three and four feet (91-122 cm) in length. They are **normally tan or yellowish in background color with dark blotches down the back and smaller dark spots on the sides. They have a distinct dark stripe that extends across their head and down through the eyes.** The young are similar in appearance with the eye stripe being the best distinguishing characteristic.

Similar Species:

As noted under the Western Rattlesnake account, the Gopher Snake is sometimes mistaken for a rattlesnake because it will expand its jaws to make its head more diamond-shaped and vibrate its tail when agitated. However, the Gopher Snake has a long tail that tapers to a point, lacks rattles and has a narrower head and overall body proportions. Young Gopher Snakes and Racers are often confused because they have similar background colors with dark blotches, but the young Racer lacks the dark eye stripe and has a relatively larger eye than the Gopher Snake.

Distribution:

Gopher Snakes extend throughout the valleys of western Oregon, between the Coast Range and the Cascade Mountains at elevations below about 2,000 feet (610 m). They occur throughout eastern Washington up to 2,614 feet (797 m) near Bishop, Whitman County, and in eastern Oregon at elevations below about 5,500 feet (1,676 m).

Habits and Habitat:

Gopher Snakes occur in a variety of habitats from relatively dry desert regions to more moist agricultural regions. They may occur in drier more open forests but are seldom found in moist forests. They most commonly seek refuge under rocks, under various types of debris or in rodent burrows. They winter in communal den sites in rocks or burrows that may be shared with other snakes such as the Western Rattlesnake, Racer and Striped Whipsnake, but they are not found

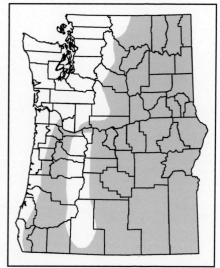

Adult (Lake County, Oregon)
Photo by Robert M. Storm

Great Basin Gopher Snake (Denio Junction, Nevada)
Photo by William P. Leonard

aggregated in large numbers.

They first emerge from wintering dens in late March or April and soon disperse away from these dens. In early spring, they are most active during the middle of the day, but are most often seen during mid-morning or evening in summer months. They are prone to crawl out on paved roads in the morning or evening in order to absorb heat from the pavement, and one should learn to watch for this to avoid killing them. The Gopher Snake is an active forager that seeks its prey by investigating burrows, brush, rocks or debris in search of a wide range of mostly small mammals and birds and their young. It is a constrictor which captures its prey by striking and grasping with its teeth, and then quickly wrapping the prey in coils of its body, killing the prey by suffocation.

Gopher Snakes mate in the spring and the females normally lay three to eight eggs in early summer. Not much is known concerning preferred sites for deposition of the eggs, but it is generally thought to be in burrows or deep in rocky crevices. Young are normally first seen in September or October.

As noted earlier, when Gopher Snakes are alarmed, they typically expand their jaws to form a more diamond-shaped head, hiss loudly and vibrate their tails. However, they typically calm down rapidly and are not difficult snakes to handle.

Remarks:

There are several subspecies of the Gopher Snake, but only two occur in our region. The Pacific Gopher Snake (*P. c. catenifer*) occurs in the western valleys, while the Great Basin Gopher Snake (*P. c. deserticola*) occurs throughout eastern Washington and Oregon.

In general, snakes should not be captured and kept in captivity as pets since this depletes wild populations and often results in neglect of the captive individuals. However, for teachers, scout leaders and other adults attempting to teach proper attitudes toward snakes, the Gopher Snake represents a good species for handling. It typically has a mild disposition and rapidly calms down after the initial encounter, normally not attempting to strike. Its constricting nature causes it to coil around one's hand or arm, making it easy to handle. After such handling to demonstrate that snakes are not "slimy" and offensive, the snake should be released at its original capture site.

Pacific Gopher Snake (Jackson County, Oregon)

Photo by William P. Leonard

Juvenile Great Basin Gopher Snake (Columbia National Wildlife Refuge)

Photo by William R. Radke

Albino Pacific Coast Gopher Snake (Benton County, Oregon)

Photo by Robert M. Storm

WESTERN GROUND SNAKE
Sonora semiannulata Baird and Girard

Description:

T he Western Ground Snake is **one of our smallest snakes** with individuals seldom exceeding 15 inches (38.1 cm) in total length. The coloration in this snake is highly variable, **but two basic patterns occur as follows: Banded individuals having black saddles down the back with orange between the saddles and unbanded individuals showing solid olive to tan above,** but usually having a faint orange stripe down the back. Regardless of the overall color pattern, this species can best be distinguished by a close inspection of the **scales on the sides where the base of each scale is black.**

Similar Species:

Unbanded Western Ground Snakes with a dorsal stripe may be confused with a small garter snake. Garter snakes have rough keeled scales while the scales of the ground snake are smooth.

Distribution:

The Western Ground Snake is known to occur only in a restricted area of southeastern Oregon. It is small and secretive so that its range may be more extensive than collection records indicate. Most of the records for this species outside of the Southwest occur in southwestern Idaho.

Habits and Habitat:

The apparent scarcity and difficulty of capturing Western Ground Snakes limit our understanding of their habitat and life history requirements. They are found in arid low-elevation regions (probably below 4,000 feet or 1,220 m) that have at least some sandy or loose soils. They can also be found in rocky areas, but small mammal or large invertebrate burrows are probably their main source of escape cover. This conclusion was reached because one of us (Diller) has observed them emerging from burrows but has seldom found them by turning rocks. It is thought that they are primarily nocturnal but they can be observed on the surface during late evening. They are taken by Red-tailed Hawks which also indicates daytime activity. They can be collected by walking through appropriate

Orange and black banded morph (Malheur County, Oregon)
Photo by Robert M. Storm

Red-striped morph (Owyhee County, Idaho)
Photo by William P. Leonard

habitat at sunset, but no technique is likely to produce many captures.

Little is known of their foraging and food habits. Small invertebrates such as spiders, centipedes and various insects probably make up most of their diet. As with other aspects of this species, little is known about their reproduction. The small samples available indicate they usually lay four eggs.

Remarks:

There are no recognized subspecies of the Western Ground Snake. Studies in southwest Idaho indicated that this was one of the rarest snakes and it is also likely the rarest in the Northwest. More work is needed to identify its habitat requirements since its apparent scarcity could make it vulnerable to extinction.

Orange and black
banded morph (Idaho)

Photo by Charles R. Peterson

Gray and black banded
morph (Idaho)

Photo by Jon Beck

Red-striped morph
(Idaho)

Photo by Jon Beck

PACIFIC COAST AQUATIC GARTER SNAKE
Thamnophis atratus (Kennicott)

Synonymous Names:
Western Aquatic Garter Snake, *T. couchii* (see remarks)

Description:
In Oregon, Pacific Coast Aquatic Garter Snakes usually have **8 upper labial scales (7th longer than 6th), 10 lower labial scales, 19 or 21 dorsal scale rows at midbody,** 138-171 ventrals, and 74-94 subcaudals. They have **internasal scales that are longer than wide and pointed anteriorly.** They are fairly slender, medium-sized snakes, reaching a maximum length of about 33 inches (84 cm) in Oregon. They have a relatively narrow head **with a pointed snout.** In Oregon, the **dorsal ground color is pale gray. Two rows of alternating dark spots** occur on each side and may be fused in large snakes. A **narrow, faint, vertebral stripe may be present but often is confined to the neck.** Dull, yellow, lateral stripes also may be present. The **ventral surface is light colored, usually unmarked, and tinted with pink or purple posteriorly.** Females grow longer than males but have relatively shorter tails and fewer ventral and caudal scales. As with all garter snakes, the eyes have round pupils, the dorsal scales are keeled, and the anal scale is undivided.

Similar Species:
Because the range of the Pacific Coast Aquatic Garter Snake overlaps with the other three species of garter snakes that occur in Oregon (the Western Terrestrial Garter Snake, the Northwestern Garter Snake, and the Common Garter Snake), these species may be confused with one another. Please refer to Table 1 on page 160 for a summary of the scalation and characteristics that distinguish these species.

Distribution:
The Pacific Coast Aquatic Garter Snake ranges from southwestern Oregon to northwestern California and south, about half-way down the California coast. In Oregon, they are known from Coos, Curry, Douglas, Jackson, and Josephine counties. In southwestern Oregon, they occur at relatively low elevations, but in California they have been recorded from sea level up to 6,240 feet (1,920 m) in elevation.

134

Adult (Jackson County, Oregon)

Photo by William P. Leonard

Adult (Jackson County, Oregon)

Photo by William P. Leonard

Adult (Jackson County, Oregon)

Photo by William P. Leonard

Habits and Habitat:

This species has been described as the most aquatic snake in the Northwest. They occur along permanent rivers and streams with exposed boulders and riparian vegetation. Look for them during the day, basking on boulders in the water or along the banks. Breeding takes place from late March to April, and 3 to 12 young are born from August through October.

Pacific Coast Garter Snakes feed on fish (sculpins and small trout), hylid and ranid frogs and tadpoles, toads, plethodontid salamanders, and aquatic salamanders and their larvae. Very young aquatic garter snakes are primarily sit-and-wait foragers, ambushing prey from rocks in the shallow edge waters. Adults actively forage in fast-moving, relatively deep (e.g., 19 inch, 0.5 m) water. Juveniles use both foraging modes to hunt for prey in shallow riffles and edgewaters.

Like other snakes that spend time in exposed streamsides, these snakes are wary and may bite if captured. They commonly escape by diving into water and hiding beneath rocks on the bottom or under exposed tree roots. A Racer (*Coluber constrictor*) was observed attempting to eat an adult Pacific Coast Garter Snake.

Remarks:

Three subspecies of Pacific Coast Aquatic Garter Snakes are currently recognized; only the Oregon Garter Snake (*T. a. hydrophilus*) occurs in Oregon. In the past, this subspecies has been classified as a Northwestern Garter Snake (*Thamnophis ordinoides*), a Western Terrestrial Garter Snake (*Thamnophis elegans*), and, most recently, as a Western Aquatic Garter Snake (*Thamnophis couchii*). Pacific Coast Aquatic Garter Snakes are known to hybridize (interbreed) with both Western Aquatic Garter Snakes and Two-striped Garter Snakes (*Thamnophis hammondii*) in parts of California.

Adult (Jackson County, Oregon)

Photo by John S. Applegarth

Adult eating a fish (Siskiyou County, California)

Photo by John S. Applegarth

Adult (Curry County, Oregon)

Photo by Robert M. Storm

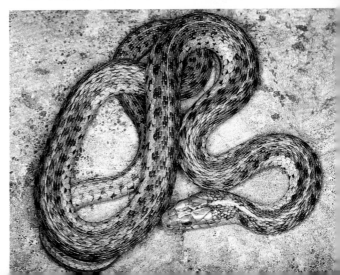

WESTERN TERRESTRIAL GARTER SNAKE
Thamnophis elegans (Baird and Girard)

Description:

Because of the great variation in the pattern and color of Western Terrestrial Garter Snakes, scalation characters are most useful in positively identifying this species. These snakes usually possess **10 lower labial scales and 8 upper labial scales** (occasionally 7, rarely 9). The 6th and 7th upper labials are often higher than wide in terrestrial subspecies because of enlarged salivary glands. The **internasals are usually broader than long and are not pointed anteriorly. The dorsal scale rows number 19 or 21 at midbody.** Ventral scale numbers vary from 146 to 185 and subcaudal numbers vary from 64 to 101.

Coloration and pattern are highly variable between the three subspecies of Western Terrestrial Garter Snakes that occur in Washington and Oregon. The dorsal ground color of the Mountain Garter Snake (*T. e. elegans*) is black or dark brown with light flecks. The vertebral stripe is bright yellow or orange, straight-edged, and wide, covering the median row and half of each adjacent row of dorsal scales. The lateral stripes are distinct, dull yellow, and confined to the 2nd and 3rd dorsal scale rows. The ventral surface is pale, rarely with black markings.

The dorsal ground color of the Coast Garter Snake (*T. e. terrestris*) is olive or reddish brown. The vertebral stripe is bright yellow, straight edged, and wide, covering the median row and half of each adjacent row of dorsal scales. The lateral stripes are yellow with varying amounts of red pigment. Two alternating rows of black spots occur between the stripes, and the skin between the scales may be suffused with red pigment. The chin is light colored, and the rest of the ventral surface is pale green or blue, with red flecks.

The dorsal color of the Wandering Garter Snake (*T. e. vagrans*) is light gray to light brown. A dull yellow vertebral stripe is usually present, narrow (largely confined to the median dorsal scale row), and uneven (invaded by the upper of two series of small black spots in the dorsolateral areas). The lateral stripes are dull yellow, located on the 2nd and 3rd dorsal scale rows, and sometimes are indistinct. The ventral surface is light gray with black flecking distributed irregularly or concentrated medially. Melanistic (dark) individuals are known from populations in the Puget Sound Area, southeastern Washington, and eastern

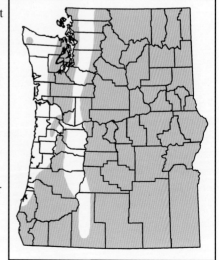

Melanistic *T. e. vagrans* (Pierce County, Washington)
Photo by William P. Leonard

Melanistic *T. e. vagrans* showing 8 upper labials (Pierce County, Washington)
Photo by William P. Leonard

Oregon. Some individuals are almost totally black.

Western Terrestrial Garter Snakes can reach lengths of up to 43 inches (107 cm) in total length. Females are larger than males but have relatively shorter tails and fewer ventral and subcaudal scales.

Similar Species:

Because the range of the Western Terrestrial Garter Snake overlaps with the other three species of garter snakes that occur in Washington or Oregon, these species may be confused with one another. Please refer to Table 1 on page 160 for a summary of the scalation and characteristics that distinguish these species. Over most of its range in eastern Washington and eastern Oregon, the only species with which it is likely to be confused is the Common Garter Snake.

Distribution:

Western Terrestrial Garter Snakes are widespread in western North America. They range from British Columbia south into California, east to New Mexico, and north to southwestern Saskatchewan. Isolated populations occur both north and south (in Mexico) of the main range. These snakes are found in most of Washington and Oregon, but are absent along most of the coast, the crest of the Cascade Mountains, and part of south-central Oregon. They occur from sea level in the San Juan Islands in Washington up to 8,400 feet (2,560 m) on Steens Mountain, Harney County, Oregon, and to 7,300 feet (2,225 m) in the Wallowa Mountains, Wallowa County, Oregon, and to 4,085 feet (1,246 m) near Rimrock Lake, Yakima County, Washington. The most widely distributed subspecies is the Wandering Garter Snake (*T. e. vagrans*) which occurs throughout most of Washington and eastern Oregon. The Mountain Garter Snake (*T. e. elegans*) occurs in the mountains and valleys of southwestern Oregon. The Coast Garter Snake (*T. e. terrestris*) enters the extreme southwestern corner of Oregon.

Habits and Habitat:

Western Terrestrial Garter Snakes inhabit a wide diversity of areas, including grasslands, shrublands, woodlands, and open forest. Although they sometimes may be found far from water, they are most commonly found near water, marshes, springs, streams, rivers, ponds, lakes, and even the ocean. Wandering Garter Snakes are terrestrial and semiaquatic, whereas the Mountain and Coast Garter Snakes are more terrestrial. Western Terrestrial Garter Snakes typically den in rocky areas, sometimes in large numbers (100s). In eastern Washington, they are known to share den sites with Rubber Boas, Racers, and Common Garter Snakes. Summer activity areas may be close to the denning areas or may be several miles (kilometers) away, requiring spring and fall migrations.

Throughout much of their range in Washington and Oregon, the activity season ranges from March through September or October. Breeding usually occurs in the spring, following emergence from hibernation. The males stay in the denning area for a longer period than the females. In the cooler portions of their range, females do not reproduce every year. Females may aggregate

140

T. e. vagrans (Thurston County Washington)
Photo by William P. Leonard

T. e. vagrans (Harney County, Oregon)
Photo by William P. Leonard

during the later part of their gestation period (July to September). During this period the pregnant females are relatively inactive, spending most of their time thermoregulating, presumably to optimize development of their young. Four to 19 young are born sometime between July and September. Several cases of fall breeding have been reported.

These snakes are primarily active during the day, but may occasionally be active on warm evenings as well. They are most easily observed when basking in the morning. When it is warm enough to do so, they usually select body temperatures near 86° F (30° C).

Western Terrestrial Garter Snakes can be very abundant. They can persist in areas disturbed by humans, and often use human structures (e.g., roadbeds, bridges, building foundations) as den sites.

Western Terrestrial Garter Snakes have one of the most diverse diets of any snake. Depending on the location, they will forage terrestrially, in trees, and/or in fresh and saltwater. They will feed on slugs, snails, leeches, earthworms, fish, salamanders and their larvae, frogs and tadpoles, lizards, snakes, birds, small mammals (including mice, voles, and even bats), and carrion. What they eat is largely influenced by what is available, but studies have demonstrated genetically based differences among populations in prey preferences. Although they simply swallow small prey items alive, they may coil around larger prey items, such as rodents, to subdue them. Their enlarged posterior teeth and a toxic saliva help to subdue and digest their prey but do not pose a danger to humans.

Western Terrestrial Garter Snakes avoid predators or defend themselves in a variety of ways. Their coloration and pattern help conceal them. If disturbed, they may try to crawl away, but often stop abruptly after moving only a few feet. Members of some subspecies will flee on land while others will enter the water, where they may dive or remain at the surface. If captured, garter snakes will usually release the contents from their cloaca (feces and uric acid) and musk glands. Garter snakes in some areas will also bite to defend themselves. Birds are probably the most important predators on this species.

Remarks:

Six subspecies of the Western Terrestrial Garter Snake are currently recognized, three of which occur in Washington and Oregon, the Mountain Garter Snake (*T. e. elegans*), the Coast Garter Snake (*T. e. terrestris*), and the Wandering Garter Snake (*T. e. vagrans*). Some herpetologists recognize a fourth subspecies, the Klamath Garter Snake (*T. e. biscutatus*), in south-central Oregon, whereas other herpetologists consider the Western Terrestrial Garter Snakes in this area to be intergrades between the Wandering and Mountain Garter Snakes. The very dark populations of *T. elegans* in Puget Sound were considered a distinct subspecies (*T. e. nigrescens*) in the past.

142

T. e. biscutatus
(Lake County, Oregon)

Photo by John S. Applegarth

T. e. elegans (Jackson
County, Oregon)

Photo by John S. Applegarth

T. e. terrestris
(Curry County, Oregon)

Photo by Robert M. Storm

NORTHWESTERN GARTER SNAKE
Thamnophis ordinoides (Baird and Girard)

Description:

Northwestern Garter Snakes **have the most variable scalation of any garter snake in the Northwest.** They usually have **7 upper labial scales per side (rarely 6 or 8), 8 lower labial scales (frequently 9, rarely 7 or 10), 17 mid-dorsal scale rows (rarely 15 or 19),** 136-162 ventral scales, and 49-72 subcaudal scales.

With respect to color pattern, Northwestern Garter Snakes are **considered to be the most variable snake in Washington or Oregon.** Although populations may have a most common color pattern, a wide range of variation is present within many populations. A great deal of variation in color and pattern can occur even within the same litter of snakes. The dorsal ground color may be black, gray, olive, or some shade of brown, sometimes with a bluish or greenish cast. A well-defined, vertebral stripe is usually present, but may be faint, broken, or absent. Its color may be red, orange, yellow, white, or blue. Yellow or white lateral stripes, located on the 2nd and 3rd dorsal scale rows, occur commonly, but may be faint or absent. Two alternating rows of black spots may occur between the dorsal and lateral stripes (most apparent in juveniles). These spots do not invade the dorsal stripe (as often happens in *T. elegans*). Light flecks also may occur between the stripes. The ventral coloration may range from yellow through some shade of brown to slate gray. It usually is paler than the dorsal ground color and often contains black or red markings.

They are relatively small garter snakes, usually less than two feet (60 cm) in total length, although an individual exceeding three feet (95 cm) has been recorded. Females reach greater overall length but males have relatively longer tails. **Head size is relatively small;** head shape is variable.

Similar Species:

The range of the Northwestern Garter Snake overlaps with the other three species of garter snakes that occur in Washington or Oregon. Consequently, these four species may be confused with one another. Please refer to Table 1 on page 160 for a summary of the scalation and characteristics that distinguish these species. The relatively small head of the Northwestern Garter Snake helps in distinguishing them from the other garter snakes.

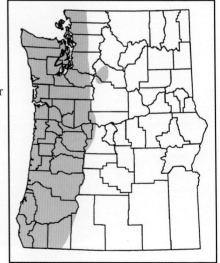

Red-striped morph
(Pacific County,
Washington)

Photo by William P. Leonard

Turquoise-striped
morph (Thurston
County, Washington)

Photo by William P. Leonard

Yellow-striped morph
(Thurston County,
Washington)

Photo by William P. Leonard

Distribution:

Northwestern Garter Snakes are found on Vancouver Island and in southwestern British Columbia, western Washington, western Oregon, and the northwestern corner of California. In Washington and Oregon, their range extends just east of the Cascade Mountains along the Columbia River and across Snoqualmie Pass to Cle Elum, Kittitas County, Washington. They can be found from sea level up to about 4,000 feet (1,219 m) in the Coast Range and to 5,500 feet (1,676 m) in the Cascade Range in Oregon, and to 4,200 feet (1,280 m) on Mt. Steel, Jefferson County, Washington.

Habits and Habitat:

Northwestern Garter Snakes are frequently associated with the coastal fog belt. They are primarily terrestrial but may be found near water. They inhabit meadows, brushy thickets, talus slopes, and clearings in forests. They hibernate in talus or in cracks in fissured rock but may show relatively low fidelity to particular den sites. They may be found in large numbers as they emerge from hibernation. In the milder portion of the range, these snakes may not communally hibernate.

They are generally active from March to October but may occasionally be observed during winter months at low elevations if the conditions are appropriate. They are diurnal and are most active on warm, sunny days. Pregnant, shedding, or digesting snakes are especially likely to bask. Breeding primarily occurs during March through April and, less often, from September through October. Most, but not all, mature females breed each year. Ovulation occurs in May or June, gestation lasts for about nine weeks, and 3-20 (typically 6-11) young are born sometime between July and October.

Northwestern Garter Snakes will forage in the rain, feeding primarily on earthworms and slugs, occasionally on snails, salamanders, and frogs.

The well-developed color polymorphism (a variety of colors and markings) in these snakes probably makes them more difficult for predators (especially birds) to detect and capture. Recent studies indicate that striped Northwestern Garter Snakes will usually crawl straight away from a predator, but that spotted or unmarked snakes often reverse direction and "freeze". If threatened, these snakes will often seek cover in dense vegetation, even if they are near water. If handled, Northwestern Garter Snakes rarely bite. However, they will usually release the contents from their cloaca (feces and uric acid) and musk glands. Red-tailed Hawks, Robins, Spotted Owls, and Steller's Jays have been observed eating Northwestern Garter Snakes in Oregon.

Remarks:

No subspecies of Northwestern Garter Snake are currently recognized. In the past, Northwestern Garter Snakes have been lumped together with the Pacific Coast Garter Snake (*T. atratus*), the Sierra Garter Snake (*T. couchii*), the Western Terrestrial Garter Snake (*T. elegans*), and the Giant Garter Snake (*T. gigas*).

Albino (Thurston
County, Washington)

Photo by William P. Leonard

Adult (Linn County,
Oregon)

Photo by John S. Applegarth

Juvenile (Thurston
County, Washington)

Photo by William P. Leonard

COMMON GARTER SNAKE
Thamnophis sirtalis (Linnaeus)

Description:

B ecause of the regional variation in the pattern and color of Common Garter Snakes, scalation characters are important in positively identifying this species. These snakes **usually possess 10 lower labial scales and 7 upper labial scales** (infrequently 8, rarely 6 or 9). The **dorsal scale rows number 19 at midbody.** Ventral scale numbers vary from 137 to 178 and subcaudal numbers vary from 52 to 97. Males average more ventral and subcaudal scales than females and have knobbed keels on dorsal scales above the vent.

Coloration and pattern are variable between and within the three subspecies of Common Garter Snakes that occur in Washington and Oregon. The Red-spotted Garter Snake (*T. s. concinnus*) has a black, dorsal ground color. The top and sides of the head are red or chestnut brown. The vertebral stripe is bright yellow and relatively wide (covering the median row and half of each adjacent row of dorsal scales). Although lateral stripes are usually absent, narrow, irregular, pale gray stripes or markings may occur on the 2nd and 3rd scale rows. A series of large red blotches or crescents occurs on each side. The ventral coloration is light anteriorly, becoming darker posteriorly. Black pigmentation may extend from the sides of the body onto the ventral surface.

The Valley Garter Snake (*T. s. fitchi*) has a black or slaty dorsal ground color. The tops and sides of the head are dark gray or black. The vertebral stripe is bright yellow, straight-edged, and covers the median row and half of each adjacent row of dorsal scales. Pale gray or yellow lateral stripes occur on the 2nd and 3rd scale rows. A series of small red blotches occurs on the lower half of the dorsolateral area on each side. The chin is light colored. The belly is yellow-green to yellow-blue, becoming darker posteriorly. Black markings do not occur on the ventral surface. Slate-gray individuals are known from within the caldera of Crater Lake, Oregon.

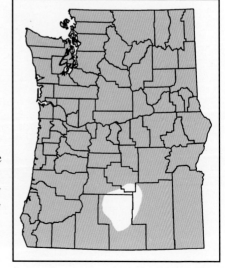

The Puget Sound Garter Snake (*T. s. pickeringii*) has a black dorsal ground color. The top and sides of the head are black. The vertebral stripe is yellow-green or turquoise, and usually narrow (covering only the median row of dorsal scales). Irregular, narrow, lateral stripes occur on the 2nd scale rows. Lateral and dorsal stripes are

T. s. fitchi showing 7 upper labials (Okanogan County, Washington)
Photo by William P. Leonard

T. s. fitchi (Okanogan County, Washington)
Photo by William P. Leonard

usually the same color. A series of small red blotches or crescents (limited to the skin between the scales) may occur on each side. The chin is light colored. The ventral coloration grades from light green or blue anteriorly to solid black posteriorly. Common Garter Snakes are relatively large, heavy-bodied garter snakes, with a moderate-sized head and relatively large eyes. They can reach lengths of up to 52 inches (132 cm) in total length. Females are larger than males but have relatively shorter tails.

Similar Species:

Because the range of the Common Garter Snake overlaps with the other three species of garter snakes that occur in Washington or Oregon, these species may be confused with one another. Please refer to Table 1 on page 160 for a summary of the scalation and characteristics that distinguish these species.

Distribution:

Common Garter Snakes are the most wide-ranging reptile in North America. They range from Canada to Mexico and from the Pacific to Atlantic coasts but are absent from most of the southwestern United States. The Common Garter Snake occurs from sea level up to 6,000 feet (1,850 m) on Mount Hood, Oregon and to 5,700 feet (1,738 m) near Obstruction Peak, Olympic National Park, Clallam County, Washington. The Valley Garter Snake (*T. s. fitchi*) occurs throughout Washington and Oregon, except for the coastal areas of Washington and northern Oregon, and the arid central portions of these states. The Red-spotted Garter Snake (*T. s. concinnus*) occurs in northwestern Oregon, southwestern Washington, and along the western coast of Washington. The Puget Sound Garter Snake (*T. s. pickeringii*) occurs in the Puget Sound area and on the Olympic Peninsula, except for a narrow belt along the Pacific Coast.

Habits and Habitat:

Common Garter Snakes inhabit a wide diversity of areas, including grasslands, shrublands, and forests. They are usually found near wetlands (lakes, ponds, marshes, sloughs, streams, meadows, etc.), even in areas disturbed by humans. In the drier, eastern portions of Washington and Oregon, they are more closely associated with water; in the moister, western portions of these states, they also may be found in open valleys and deep, coniferous forests, some distance from water. Look for them under cover objects, such as logs and rocks, basking along the banks of water courses, or swimming in the water. They typically overwinter in rocky areas. In eastern Washington, they are known to share denning sites with Rubber Boas, Racers, and Western Terrestrial Garter Snakes. Their den sites may be close to their summer activity areas or may be many miles (kilometers) away, requiring spring and fall migrations. They can be very abundant (100s) at these den sites and in their summer foraging areas (e.g., a wet meadow with a stream).

T. s. pickeringii (Pierce County, Washington)

Photo by William P. Leonard

T. s. pickeringii (Thurston County, Washington)

Photo by William P. Leonard

T. s. pickeringii (Thurston County, Washington)

Photo by William P. Leonard

Throughout much of their range in Washington and Oregon, the activity season ranges from March through September or October. In the milder portion of their range, males may emerge on warm days during the winter. Breeding usually occurs in the spring, following emergence from hibernation, but fall breeding also has been observed. Some adult females do not reproduce every year. The males find the females by airborne scent and by trailing. Up to 100 males may simultaneously court a single female, forming a "snake ball". The males semen causes formation of a copulatory plug in the female's cloaca, which prevents her from breeding with other males, at least for a few days. Because females can store sperm in their reproductive tracts, multiple paternity can occur. Ovulation occurs in May or early June. Females may aggregate during the later part of their gestation period (July to August). The young are born sometime between July and September. The number of young usually ranges from 10 to 18, but litter sizes up to 80 are known to occur. As with other species of snakes, larger females generally have higher numbers of young. Males typically reach maturity in 1 to 2 years, females in 2 to 3 years, but these times are lengthened in cooler areas. The maximum recorded longevity in captivity is 10 years.

These snakes are primarily active during the day, but may occasionally be active in the evenings. They are most easily observed when basking in the morning or when foraging in riparian areas. When it is warm enough to do so, garter snakes usually select body temperatures near 86° F (30° C), especially if they are pregnant, digesting prey, or in the process of molting their skin.

Common Garter Snakes have a diverse diet which largely reflects the availability of prey. Young snakes primarily feed on earthworms. Adults usually feed on amphibians (larvae and adults) or small fish, less often on earthworms, slugs, leeches, snails, birds, and small mammals, and rarely on insects, spiders, or small snakes.

Common Garter Snakes avoid predators and defend themselves in several ways. Their coloration and pattern help to conceal them from predators. If disturbed they usually will retreat into the water or under cover. If they are in the open or are unable to escape, they will often flatten their body, making their red marks more visible. Like many snakes, they may also flatten their heads and may strike. If captured, garter snakes will usually release the contents from their cloaca (feces and uric acid) and musk glands. Garter snakes in some areas will also bite to defend themselves. Birds are probably the most important predators on these snakes, but some predaceous fish, large amphibians, some snakes and mammals, and even predaceous beetles may eat them.

Remarks:

Eleven subspecies of Common Garter Snakes are currently recognized, three of which occur in Washington and Oregon, the Valley Garter Snake (*T. s. fitchi*), the Red-spotted Garter Snake (*T. s. concinnus*), and the Puget Sound Garter Snake (*T. s. pickeringii*). In the past, a fourth subspecies, the Three-

T. s. concinnus (Clark County, Washington)

Photo by William P. Leonard

T. s. concinnus (Clallam County, Washington)

Photo by William P. Leonard

striped Garter Snake (*T. s. trilineata*), was recognized by some herpetologists. It ranged from the Puget Sound lowlands west to Grays Harbor, Washington, and north into British Columbia. Although somewhat different than the Puget Sound Garter Snakes from the southeastern portion of Puget Sound, it is now classified with them as *T. s. pickeringii*. The taxonomic relationships of Common Garter Snakes from the western portion of Washington require further study.

WESTERN RATTLESNAKE
Crotalus viridis Rafinesque

Description:

The Western Rattlesnake is **our only truly venomous snake** and is readily identified by the **presence of "rattles" (modified scales) on the tip of the tail,** enabling it to produce a buzzing sound when agitated. This snake also has a unique body shape with a **broad diamond-shaped head and a relatively robust thick body.** The tail is short and lacks the usual taper seen in most snakes. In rare cases where the rattles are missing, the tail is very short and has a blunt amputated look. The **basic body color varies from greenish to tan with a series of dark blotches down the dorsal surface.** Adult snakes typically reach 30-40 inches (76-102 cm) in total length with the males averaging larger than the females.

If the string of rattles is intact, it is an indication of the number of times the snake has shed (undergone ecdysis), which reflects growth and age but cannot be used to accurately estimate age. Typically, an individual will shed two or three times in its first summer of growth with a reduced frequency in subsequent years, but there is a high degree of individual variation. The string of rattles seldom remains intact for more than three or four years so that most older snakes have a broken string. Young are born with a pre-button (cap-like scale) which is usually shed, forming a button, within the first week following birth. At this point the young snake is capable of producing an audible weak buzzing sound.

Similar Species:

There are no other species of snakes that can readily be confused with a rattlesnake if one is examining the snake objectively. However, the fear and anxiety often associated with this species cause people to mistake the Gopher Snake for a rattlesnake. The Gopher Snake superficially resembles a rattlesnake because both species have dark dorsal blotches on a lighter ground color. In addition, the Gopher Snake expands its jaws to make its head more diamond-shaped and vibrates its tail when it is agitated. This tail vibration may produce an audible "buzzing" sound if the snake is in dry brush or leaves, increasing the potential for a

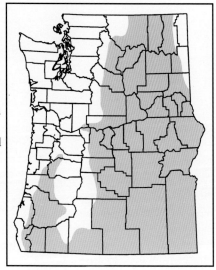

C. v. oreganus (Jackson County, Oregon)
Photo by John S. Applegarth

C. v. lutosus (Harney County, Oregon)
Photo by Robert M. Storm

mistaken identity. However, the long tapering tail, small head and more slender body of the Gopher Snake readily distinguish it from a rattlesnake. If one has an opportunity to safely examine a rattlesnake at close range, it can also be distinguished from all other Northwestern snakes by the presence of facial pits (heat-sensing organs), located on each side of the head, midway between the nostril and the eye. Juvenile racers are also frequently mistaken for rattlesnakes.

Distribution:

The Western Rattlesnake occurs in eastern Washington up to 2,942 feet (897 m) along the Tucannon River, Columbia County, Washington and in Oregon at elevations below about 7,500 feet (2,286 m). In Oregon, it also occurs in valleys west of the Cascade Mountains, but is probably absent from the Willamette Valley north of McMinnville and Salem. A few isolated dens occur in Coast Range and Cascades foothills south of these towns, in the Willamette Valley.

Habits and Habitat:

The Western Rattlesnake is usually found in drier regions with low or sparse vegetation. They are most often found associated with rocky areas. They are known for aggregating in large numbers at communal den sites, which are typically in talus or fissures in rock. They commonly use rocky areas for basking and escape cover, but may also use rodent burrows as refuge sites. Rattlesnakes can usually first be seen around the entrance of the den or hibernaculum in late March and April. As spring progresses, they disperse onto their summer range. During the early spring when the weather is cool (60°-70° F.) but sunny, rattlesnakes can be observed most commonly during the middle of the day. When daytime temperatures get hot during the summer, rattlesnakes normally are seen only during mid-morning and evening hours. Rattlesnakes become highly nocturnal in southern regions, but night time temperatures are usually too cool to permit much nocturnal activity in our region.

The Western Rattlesnake is a typical sit-and-wait ambush predator that feeds mostly on small mammals, but will also take birds, lizards and amphibians. They strike their prey and inject venom through a pair of hinged fangs. Typically, the prey is released following the strike and the snake then follows a scent trail to locate the immobilized dead or dying animal.

When rattlesnakes are disturbed by a human presence, they normally respond by either remaining motionless to avoid detection, moving away and seeking cover, or assuming a defensive posture with their body coiled in a striking position, while emitting a buzzing sound produced by high frequency vibrations of their rattles. If a person backs away from a rattlesnake in a defensive posture, the snake will almost always retreat and seek cover. Occasionally, rattlesnakes will try to defend themselves by hiding their heads under their body coils. Rattlesnakes are normally capable of striking only about half of their body length or less, but will seldom strike unless provoked by a contin-

156

C. v. oreganus (Klickitat County, Washington)
Photo by William P. Leonard

C. v. oreganus at den (Columbia National Wildlife Refuge)
Photo by William R. Radke

ued close proximity threat. Most cases of snakebite are the results of someone's attempting to handle a rattlesnake.

Western Rattlesnakes are capable of mating at any time during their seasonal period of activity, but most mating probably occurs in the spring or fall. The pattern of mating activity apparently varies between regions, but the details are not known for most populations. Eggs are retained and develop inside the female, with three to twelve young born in late August or September. Females normally do not produce young every year, but there is considerable variation in the frequency of reproduction, probably depending on the availability of prey animals.

Remarks:

The Western Rattlesnake occurs as two subspecies in the Northwest. The Northern Pacific Rattlesnake (*C. v. oreganus*) occurs in eastern Washington, the northern and western portion of eastern Oregon and in the western Oregon valleys. The Great Basin Rattlesnake (*C. v. lutosus*) occurs in the southeastern portion of eastern Oregon.

There is a great deal of misinformation concerning the threat that the Western Rattlesnake represents to humans. Many defensive strikes by rattle-snakes are "dry bites" with no venom being injected. This leads some to believe that the venom of a rattlesnake is little worse than a bad "bee sting". On the other extreme, some people feel compelled to carry a weapon in snake country and kill every rattlesnake seen. The venom of the Western Rattlesnake is dangerous and will cause serious tissue damage but seldom results in death. The rattlesnake should be viewed as part of the natural environment that should be respected but treated with caution. When a rattlesnake is encountered in its natural environment, away from homes and children, one should simply stay a safe distance away and leave the snake unmolested.

Juvenile *C. v. oreganus* (Benton County, Washington)
Photo by William P. Leonard

C. v. oreganus after eating a ground squirrel (Wasco County, Oregon)
Photo by William P. Leonard

TABLE 1. CHARACTERISTICS OF NORTHWEST GARTER SNAKES

CHARACTERISTIC	PACIFIC COAST AQUATIC GARTER SNAKE *Thamnophis atratus*	WESTERN TERRESTRIAL GARTER SNAKE *Thamnophis elegans*	NORTHWESTERN GARTER SNAKE *Thamnophis ordinoides*	COMMON GARTER SNAKE *Thamnophis sirtalis*
Upper Labial Scales	8	usually 8 (occasionally 7, rarely 9)	usually 7 (rarely 6 or 8)	usually 7 (occasionally 8)
Lower Labial Scales	10	usually 10	usually 8 or 9	usually 10
Internasal Scales	longer than wide and pointed anteriorly	usually broader than long and not pointed anteriorly	*	*
Chin Shields	rear pair usually longer than front pair	both pairs about equal in length	*	rear pair usually longer than front pair
Dorsal Scale Rows (at midbody)	19 or 21	19 or 21	usually 17 (occasionally 19)	19
Head Shape/Size	relatively narrow with pointed snout	moderate	relatively small	moderate
Vertebral Stripe	if present, narrow, faint and often confined to neck	usually present; color usually yellow, sometimes orange or brown	usually present but may be faint, broken, or absent; yellow, red, orange, or blue	usually present; yellow, greenish-yellow, or turquoise
Lateral Stripes	if present, dull yellow	usually occur on 2nd and 3rd dorsal scale rows	usually present, may be faint or absent; 2nd and 3rd dorsal scale rows	usually present; yellow, greenish-yellow, turquoise, or gray; 2nd and 3rd dorsal scale rows

* Not a defining characteristic.

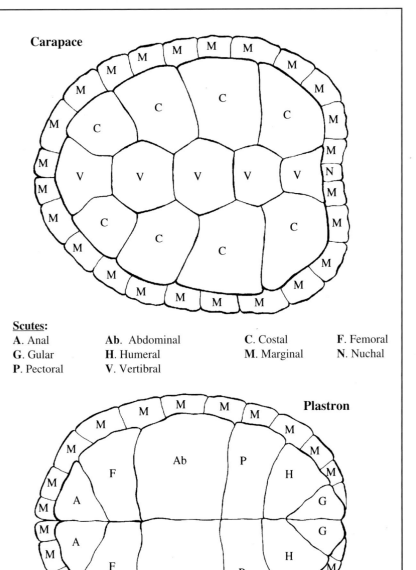

Carapace

Scutes:
A. Anal   Ab. Abdominal   C. Costal   F. Femoral
G. Gular   H. Humeral   M. Marginal   N. Nuchal
P. Pectoral   V. Vertibral

Plastron

Figure 1. Turtle shell from above and below

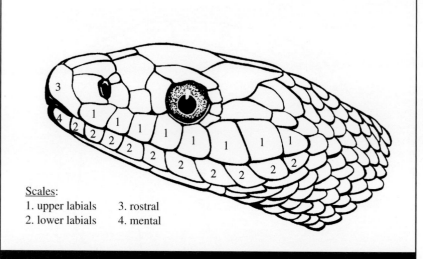

Scales:
1. upper labials   3. rostral
2. lower labials   4. mental

Figure 2. Head of snake from side *(Thamnophis atratus)*

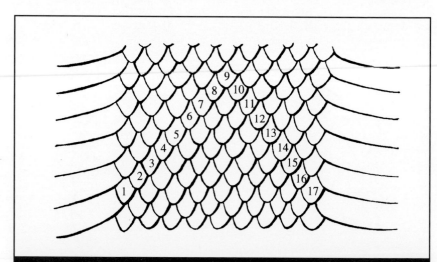

Figure 3. Counting scale rows on snakes *(T. ordinoides)*

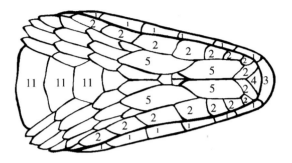

Scales:
1. upper labials
2. lower labials
3. rostral
4. mental
5. chin shields
6. internasals

7. prefrontals
8. supraoculars
9. frontal
10. parietals
11. ventrals (gastrosteges)

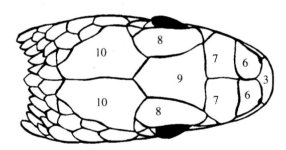

Figure 4. Head of snake from below and above *(T. sirtalis)*

163

GENERAL REFERENCES

Behler, J.L. and F.W. King. 1979. The Audubon Society Field Guide to Reptiles and Amphibians. New York: Alfred A. Knopf.

Blaustein, A.R., J.J. Beatty, D.H. Olson, and R.M. Storm. 1995. The Biology of Amphibians and Reptiles in Old-Growth Forests in the Pacific Northwest. Gen. Tec. Rep. PNW-GTR-337. U.S. Dept. of Agriculture, Forest Service, Pacific Northwest Research Station. 98pp.

Carr, Archie. 1952. Handbook of Turtles. Ithaca: Cornell University Press.

Ernst, C.H., J.E. Lovich, and R.W. Barbour. 1994. Turtles of the United States and Canada. Smithsonian Institute Press, Washington, D.C. 578pp.

Halliday, T. and K. Adler. 1986. The Encyclopedia of Reptiles and Amphibians. Facts on File. 143pp.

Johnson, M.L. 1995 (1954). Reptiles of the State of Washington. *Northwest Fauna* 3:5-79, Society for Northwestern Vertebrate Biology, Olympia, Washington.

Leonard, W.P., H.A. Brown, L.L.C. Jones, K.R. McAllister, and R.M. Storm. 1993. Amphibians of Washington and Oregon. Seattle Audubon Society.

Nussbaum, R.A., E.D. Brodie, Jr., and R.M. Storm. 1983. Amphibians and Reptiles of the Pacific Northwest. The University Press of Idaho, Moscow, Idaho.

Smith, H.M. 1946. Handbook of Lizards of the United States and Canada. Ithaca: Comstock Publishing Company.

Smith, H.M. and E.D. Brodie, Jr. 1982. Reptiles of North America. New York: Golden Press.

Stebbins, R.C. 1985. A Field Guide to Western Reptiles and Amphibians. Houghton Mifflin Co., Boston.

St. John, A.D. 1980. Knowing Oregon Reptiles. Salem (OR) Audubon Society.

Wright, A.H. and A.A. Wright. 1957. 8th printing 1989. Handbook of Snakes of the United States and Canada. Ithaca. Cornell University Press.

Zug, G.R. 1993. Herpetology: An Introductory Biology of Amphibians and Reptiles. Philadelphia: W.B. Saunders Company.

SELECTED BIBLIOGRAPHY

Blanchard, F.N. 1942. The ring-neck snakes, Genus *Diadophis*. Bull. Chicago Acad. Sci. 7:1-144.

Brodie, E.D., Jr., R.A. Nussbaum, and R.M. Storm. 1969. An egg-laying aggregation of five species of Oregon Reptiles. *Herpetologica* 25:223-227.

Brown, W.S. and W.S. Parker. 1976. Movement ecology of *Coluber constrictor* near communal hibernacula. *Copeia* 1976:225-242.

Brown, W.S., W.S. Parker, and J.A. Elder. 1974. Thermal and spatial relationships of two species of colubrid snakes during hibernation. *Herpetologica* 30:32-38.

Cadle, J.E. 1984. Molecular systematics of neotropical xenodontine snakes. III. Overview of xenodontine phylogeny and the history of New World snakes. *Copeia* 1984:641-652.

Collins, J.T. 1990. Standard common and current scientific names for North American amphibians and reptiles, third edition. Society for the Study of Amphibians and Reptiles: Herpetological Circular No. 19.

Collins, J.T. 1991. Viewpoint: a new taxonomic arrangement for some North American amphibians and reptiles. Herpetol. Rev. 22:42-43.

Cook, S.F. Jr. 1960. On the occurrence and life history of *Contia tenuis*. *Herpetologica* 16:163-173.

Corn, P.S. and R.B. Bury. 1986. Morphological variation and zoogeography of racers (*Coluber constrictor*) in the central Rocky Mountains. *Herpetologica* 42:258-264.

Cunningham, J.D. 1959. Reproduction and food of some California snakes. *Herpetologica* 15:17-19.

Fitch, H.S. 1936. Amphibians and reptiles of the Rogue River Basin, Oregon. *Amer. Midl. Nat.* 17:634-652.

Fitch, H.S. 1949. Study of snake populations in central California. *Amer. Midl. Nat.* 41:513-579.

Fitch, H.S. 1975. A demographic study of the ringneck snake (Diadophis punctatus) in Kansas. Univ. Kansas Publ. Mus. Nat. Hist., Misc. Publ. No. 62.

Fitch, H.S. 1980. *Thamnophis sirtalis.* Cat Amer Amphib Rept: 270.1-270.4.

Fitch, H.S. 1983. *Thamnophis elegans.* Cat Amer Amphib Rept: 320.1-320.4.

Fitch, H.S. 1984. *Thamnophis couchii.* Cat Amer Amphib Rept: 351.1-351.3.

Gotch, A.F. 1986. Reptiles-Their Latin Names Explained. A Guide to Animal Classification. Blanford Press. Poole, Dorset. Great Britain.

Green, H.W. 1984. Taxonomic status of the western racer, *Coluber constrictor mormon*. *J. Herpetol.* 18:210-211.

Hayes, M.P. MSC thesis on Mountain Kingsnake. California State University, Chico, California.

Hirth, H.F., R.C. Pendleton, A.C. King, and T.R. Downard. 1969. Dispersal of snakes from a hibernaculum in northwestern Utah. *Ecology* 50:332-339.

Johnson, M.L. 1939. *Lampropeltis zonata* (Blainville) in Washington State. Occas. Pap. Dept. Biol. Univ. Puget Sound 1:2-3.

Kingsbury, Bruce A. 1994. Thermal constraints and eurythermy in the lizard *Elgaria multicarinata*. *Herpetologica* 50(3):266-273.

Kirk, J.J. 1979. *Thamnophis ordinoides*. Cat Amer Amphib Rept: 233.1-233.2

Lavin-Murcio and Kenneth W. Kardong. 1995. Scents related to venom and prey as cues in poststrike trailing behavior of rattlesnakes, *Crotalus viridis oreganus*. *Herpetologica* 51(1):39-44.

Lind, A.J. and H.H. Welsh, Jr. 1994. Ontogenetic changes in foraging behaviour and habitat use by the Oregon garter snake, *Thamnophis atratus hydrophilus*. *Anim. Behav.,* 48: 1261-1273.

McAllister, K.R. 1995. Distribution of amphibians and reptiles in Washington. *Northwest Fauna* 3:81-112.

Parker, H.W. and A.G.C. Grandison. 1977. Snakes- A Natural History. Ithaca and London: British Museum (Natural History), Cornell University Press.

Parker, W. S. and W. S. Brown. 1974. Notes on the ecology of regal ringneck snakes (*Diadophis punctatus regalis*) in northern Utah. *J. Herpetol.* 8:262-263.

Perkins, C.B. 1952. Incubation period of snake eggs. *Herpetologica* 8:79.

Peters, J.A. 1964. Dictionary of Herpetology. New York and London: Hafner Publishing Company.

Rossman, D.A., N.B. Ford, and R.A. Seigel. In Press. The Garter Snakes: Evolution and Ecology. University of Oklahoma Press, Norman, OK.

Rodriguez-Robles, Javier A. 1994. Are the Duvernoy's gland secretions of colubrid snakes venoms? *Journal of Herpetology* 28(3):388-390.

Seigel, R.A., J.T. Collins, and S.S. Novak, eds. 1987. Snakes: Ecology and Evolutionary Biology. Macmillan, New York.

Shaw, C.E. and S. Campbell. 1974. Snakes of the American West. New York: Alfred A. Knopf.

Slater, J.R. 1939. *Contia tenuis* rediscovered in Washington. Occas. Pap. Dept. Biol. Univ. Puget Sound 3:5.

Slater, J.R. 1962. *Contia tenuis* discovered east of the Cascade Mountains. Occas. Pap. Dept. Biol. Univ. Puget Sound 22:207.

Slater, J. R. 1963. Distribution of Washington Reptiles. Occas. Pap. Dept. Biol. Univ. Puget Sound 24:212-233.

St. John, A.D. 1982. The herpetology of Curry County, Oregon. Oregon Department of Fish and Wildlife, Nongame Wildlife Program. Technical Report No. 82-2-04.

_____ 1982. The herpetology of the Wenaha Wildlife Area, Wallowa County, Oregon. ODFW, NWP. Technical Report No. 82-4-03.

_____ 1983. Status and distribution of three species of snakes in North-central Oregon. ODFW, NWP. Technical Report No. 82-03-09.

_____ 1984. The herpetology of Jackson and Josephine Counties, Oregon. ODFW, NWP. Technical Report No. 84-2-05.

_____ 1984. The herpetology of the upper John Day River drainage, Oregon. ODFW, NWP. Technical Report No. 84-4-05.

_____ 1985 The herpetology of the interior Umpqua River drainage, Douglas County, Oregon. ODFW, NWP. Technical Report No. 85-2-02.

_____ 1985. The herpetology of the Owyhee River drainage, Malheur County, Oregon. ODFW, NWP. Technical Report No. 85-5-03.

_____ 1987. The herpetology of the Willamette Valley, Oregon. ODFW, NWP. Technical Report No. 86-1-02.

_____ 1987. The herpetology of the oak habitat of southwestern Klamath County, Oregon. ODFW, NWP. Technical Report No. 87-3-01.

Stewart, G.R. 1977. *Charina, C. bottae.* Cat Amer Amphib Rept: 205.1-205.2.

Stickel, W.H. 1951. Distinctions between the snake genera *Contia and Eirenis. Herpetologica* 7:125-131.

Van de Velde, R.L., J. Martan, and P.L. Risley. 1962. Eggs and hatchlings of the snake *Coluber constrictor mormon* from Oregon. *Copeia* 1962:212-213.

Zweifel, R.G. 1952. Pattern variation and evolution of the mountain kingsnake, *Lampropeltis zonata. Copeia* 1952:152-16

Zweifel, R.G. 1954. Adaptation to feeding in the snake *Contia tenuis. Copeia* 1954:299-300.

Zweifel, R.G. 1974. *Lampropeltis zonata.* Cat. Amer. Amph. Rept. 174:1-4.

Glossary of Selected Terms

Aestivate or estivate: Applied to animals that become torpid during the warmest part of the year.

Anthracosaurian amphibians: Actually an early branch away from true amphibians that gave rise to mammals and reptiles. Included aquatic, semi-aquatic and terrestrial forms.

Aposematic coloration: Implies a display of an often normally hidden color or pattern by a threatened reptile to a possible predator as warning of the displayer's ability to inflict harm (e.g. by poison, venom, etc.).

Autotomy: Term applied to the self-shedding of all or part of the tail in lizards.

Bask, Basking: Exposing oneself to the sun's rays (e.g. turtles bask on emergent logs, or basking lizards are warming themselves to a preferred temperature).

Bridge: That part of the shell in turtles which connects the carapace and plastron.

Brille: A transparent scale covering the eye of a snake. It is shed along with the rest of the skin at periodic intervals.

Carapace (fig. 1): The dorsal part of the shell in turtles.

Carrion: A term used for dead and decaying flesh of animals.

Caudals: Used here to refer to the ventral scales on the underside of a snake tail. Also called subcaudals or urosteges.

Cenozoic: Literally "recent life". Geologic era lasting from 65 million years ago to present.

Chin shields (fig. 4): Usually refers to the paired elongated scales on the underside of the lower jaw of snakes. May be as one or two pairs or they may be absent.

Cloaca: A space or chamber into which empty intestinal, urinary and reproductive products. It opens to the outside by an opening variously called the anus or vent.

Clutch: Usually applied to the full number of eggs from one female in one laying, but see Multiple clutches.

Copulation: The process by which a male reptile transfers sperm to the female.

Costal (scute) (fig. 1): The scutes located lateral to the vertebrals on a turtle's carapace. Also referred to as pleural scute by some authorities.

Courtship: Applied to the various behaviors of male and female animals toward one another, usually designed to lead toward mating (copulation).

Cryptic: As applied to reptiles, usually means difficult to see or concealing (e.g., cryptic coloration).

Cytolytic: Applied to elements in snake venom that destroy tissue cells of various kinds. May be used interchangably with hemotoxic.

Denning area: Term applied to the hibernation site, usually of snakes.

Depauperate: Poorly supplied with something (e.g., "a depauperate fauna", meaning a much reduced number of animals).

Diapsid skull: Refers to lizard and snake skulls in which there are two openings on each side, posterior to the eye.

Disjunct distribution: Applied to groups such as populations, species, etc. that occur in separate areas and do not overlap.

Diurnal: Describes reptiles that are active during the day.

Dorsal scale rows (fig. 3): The longitudinal rows of scales on the back and sides of snakes. Numbers of these rows are useful in garter snake identification.

Ecdysis: The shedding of the outer dead layer of the skin. Most snakes shed their dead skin in one piece, turning it inside out as they do so. In most lizards, the old skin comes off in pieces.

Ecosystem: The system formed by a community of plants and animals interacting with their environment.

Ectotherm: Animals (e. g. reptiles) that acquire most or all of their body heat from external sources. Also called poikilothermic or "cold-blooded".

Elapids: Refers to members of the snake family Elapidae, which includes cobras, coral snakes, mambas and kraits. Contains about 180 species.

Endotherm: An animal that can maintain its body temperature through internal physiologic means. Homeotherm implies an internal ability to maintain a constant body temperature. Also known as "warm-blooded".

Envenomate: The act of introducing venom into a victim by chewing (rear-fanged snakes) or injection (rattlesnakes, cobras, etc.).

Fitness: The concept that the animal with the greatest fitness is the one with the greatest number of fertile descendants in future years.

Fossorial: Refers to digging or burrowing.

Fovea: A small area of the retina of the eye containing closely packed visual cells; usually the area of sharpest vision.

Gestation: The time between mating (fertilization of eggs) and egg-laying or birth of young.

Granular scales: These are tiny rounded scales, which do not overlap.

Gular fold: A fold of skin across the throat of a lizard (e.g., Uta) just forward of the front limb bases.

Hatchling: A young animal that has recently emerged from an egg. If recently born alive (viviparous), known as a neonate.

Hemipenes (singular Hemipenis): Paired structures located in the base of the tail of male lizards and snakes. In use, one of them can be everted (turned inside out), by blood pressure, out through the cloacal opening of the male and into the cloaca of the female, where it is held in place by various tubercles, hooks, spines, etc. while sperm-containing fluid flows along grooves into the female. The hemipenis can only be withdrawn from the female by again being inverted (turned outside in) by means of a retractor muscle.

Hemotoxic: Applied to elements in snake venom that destroy blood cells . Venoms of rattlesnakes may be largely hemotoxic.

Herpetofauna: The amphibians and reptiles of a given area.

Hibernaculum: A retreat of some sort where a reptile hibernates. Should be capable of protecting the hibernator through the coldest periods of the year.

Hibernation: A state of greatly reduced metabolic activity, usually entered into by reptiles during the cooler and colder months of the year.

Insectivore: An animal that mainly or entirely feeds on insects. Insectivores are a type of carnivore. Most lizards are largely insectivorous.

Insolation: Radiation from the sun received by a reptile.

Internasals (fig. 4): Usually paired, occasionally single, scales between the nasal scales (scales containing the two nostril openings) of snakes.

Intromittent organ: Refers to the male penis (turtles) or hemipenis (lizards and snakes) when that organ is used to transfer sperm to the female.

Jacobson's organ: Paired blind pits in the roofs of some reptiles' mouths (lizards and snakes), which relay chemical sensations of odor and taste to the brain. Also called vomeronasal organ or VNO.

Juvenile: Refers to any young reptile from hatching or birth to near adulthood. Usually applied to individuals that are obviously smaller (and younger) than typical adults. See Subadult.

Keel: In turtles, usually means a raised longitudinal ridge running all or most of the length of the carapace. In lizards and snakes, it is a longitudinal ridge on a scale.

170

Keratin: A tough hard protein that is the basic material of horns, scales and claws, and the laminae of turtle shells.

Lower labials (fig. 2): Enlarged scales bordering the sides of the lower "lip" in reptiles.

Marginal scute (figs. 2, 4): The epidermal keratin plates on the edges of the turtle carapace. They can be seen from above and below.

Mesozoic: Literally "middle life". Geologic era that lasted from 248 million years ago to 65 million years ago. Includes the Triassic (the earliest period) of 35 million years, the Jurassic of about 70 million years, and the Cretaceous (latest period) of about 80 million years.

Microhabitat: The habitat immediately surrounding a given animal (e.g., a snake moving along the ground is in a different microhabitat than a lizard basking on a large boulder).

Musk glands: As applied to snakes, paired glands in the base of the tail which open adjacent to the anus and can emit a foul-smelling substance as a defense mechanism. May also have to do with following an individual snake's trail by others of the same species.

Neurotoxic: Applied to elements in snake venom that act on the nervous system, often causing paralysis. May be the main part of certain elapid venoms.

Nocturnal: Describes reptiles that are active during the night.

Olfaction: The act of smelling.

Omnivorous: Means eating all kinds of food, including both plant and animal material.

Opisthoglyphs: Snakes with enlarged teeth of various sizes in the posterior (rear) part of the jaws. Usually associated with varying degrees of poisonous saliva. Rear-fanged snakes.

Oviparous: Applied to reptiles that produce young from eggs deposited externally by the female.

Paleozoic: Literally "ancient life". The geologic era in which life first appeared. Lasted from 590 million years ago to 248 million years ago.

Parthenogenesis: The development of an egg without fertilization by a male. May result in all female populations, such as that of *Cnemidophorus velox.*

Pectoral girdle: Bones involved with supporting the front limbs.

Pelagic: Refers to the open ocean at some distance from land.

Pelvic girdle: Bones involved with supporting the rear limbs.

Plastron: The ventral or lower shell of turtles.

Prefrontal scales (fig. 4): One or more pairs of scales located between the eyes on the dorsal part of a reptile's head.

Proteroglyph: A venomous snake having solidly fixed fangs in the anterior (front) part of the upper jaw (e.g., cobras and coral snakes).

Rudimentary: Most accurately refers to an early stage in the development of an organ or part, but is often used to refer to a vestigial part without a function.

Scalation: A general term for the numbers and arrangements of the scales of a lizard or snake.

Scute (fig. 1): A relatively large, thin horny scale on reptiles (e.g., the specialized scales covering turtles shell). Also referred to by some authorities as shields or plates.

Semiaquatic: Refers to turtles that live in the water, but emerge frequently to bask (sun) or to wander about on land. Some snakes are largely land animals, but spend much time in the water.

Sexual maturity: Age at which male animals can produce healthy sperm and at which females can produce eggs capable of being fertilized.

Sexual selection: The genetic fixation of certain characteristics in a population, because of males or females usually selecting a mate with those characteristics, over many generations.

Solenoglyph: A venomous snake having relatively long folding fans in the front part of the upper jaw (e.g., rattlesnakes and vipers).

Squamate: Refers to the Order Squamata, containing lizards, snakes and worm lizards.

Subadult: This is a somewhat subjective term applied to individual reptiles that are near adult size, but not sexually mature. In other words, they are in a late juvenile stage. See Juvenile.

Subspecies: When geographically separated populations within a species show consistent differences from one another, they may be named subspecies by adding a third name to the species name (trinomial).

Synapsid skull: Refers to the skulls of mammal-like reptiles (fossils) and of mammals, which have one opening on each side, posterior to the eye.

Talus: Usually a collection of rocks or rock fragments at the base of a cliff or on a slope.

Temporal area (skull): Sides of the head or skull posterior to the eye openings or sockets.

Territory: An area defended by an animal against trespassing by members of its own species.

Tortoise: Usually applied to terrestrial (land) turtles like box turtles and the giant turtles of the Galapagos Islands.

Transverse: Lying across or at right angles to a given direction, as the cross-bands or rings on the bodies of some snakes.

Upper labials (fig. 4): Enlarged scales bordering the sides of the upper "lips" of reptiles. Counts of these are useful in garter snake identification.

Uric acid: Excretory waste product produced by reptiles and birds, and collected in the cloaca in both groups.

Venomous: Capable of inflicting a poisonous bite.

Vent: A term used for the external opening of the cloaca.

Ventrals (fig. 4): The laterally elongated scales on the belly of a snake, between the head and anus. Also called gastrosteges.

Vestigial: Usually refers to an organ or part that no longer performs a function, but did so in an earlier evolutionary stage.

Viviparous: Applied to reptiles where the female retains the eggs within her body so that the young are born alive,

Vomeronasal organ or VNO: See Jacobson's organ.

MAP OF WASHINGTON AND OREGON COUNTIES

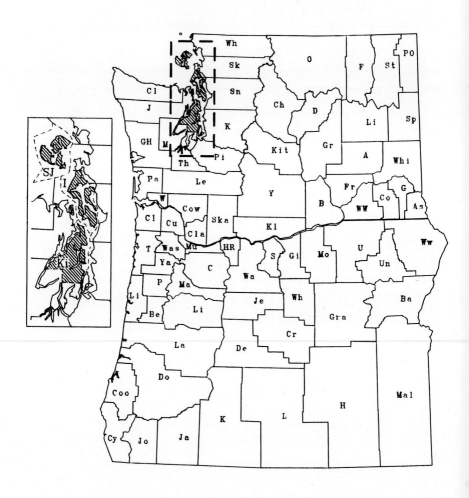

WASHINGTON COUNTIES

Adams	A
Asotin	As
Benton	B
Chelan	Ch
Clallam	Cl
Clark	Cla
Columbia	Co
Cowlitz	Cow
Douglas	D
Ferry	F
Franklin	Fr
Garfield	G
Grant	Gr
Grays Harbor	GH
Island	I
Jefferson	J
King	K
Kitsap	Ki
Kittitas	Kit
Klickitat	Kl
Lewis	Le
Lincoln	Li
Mason	M
Okanogan	O
Pacific	Pa
Pend Oreille	PO
Pierce	Pi
San Juan	SJ
Skagit	Sk
Skamania	Ska
Snohomish	Sn
Spokane	Sp
Stevens	St
Thurston	Th
Wahkiakum	W
Walla Walla	WW
Whatcom	Wh
Whitman	Whi
Yakima	Y

OREGON COUNTIES

Baker	Ba
Benton	Be
Clackamas	C
Clatsop	Cl
Columbia	Cu
Coos	Coo
Curry	Cy
Crook	Cr
Deschutes	De
Douglas	Do
Gilliam	Gi
Grant	Gra
Harney	H
Hood River	HR
Jackson	Ja
Jefferson	Je
Josephine	Jo
Klamath	Kl
Lake	L
Lane	La
Lincoln	Li
Linn	Lin
Malheur	Mal
Marion	Ma
Morrow	Mo
Multnomah	Mu
Polk	P
Sherman	S
Tillamook	T
Umatilla	U
Union	Un
Wallowa	Ww
Wasco	Wa
Washington	Was
Wheeler	Wh
Yamhill	Ya

COVER PHOTOS

Front Cover: **Western Painted Turtle**, *Chrysemys picta bellii*, Kalama River, Cowlitz County, Washington (photo by William Leonard)

Back Cover, Left: **Common (or Valley) Garter Snake**, *Thamnophis sirtalis fitchi*, Okanogan County, Washington (photo by William Leonard)

Back Cover, Center: **Western Pond Turtle**, *Clemmys marmorata*, Trinity County, California (photo by William Leonard)

Back Cover, Right: **Mojave Black-collared Lizard**, *Crotaphytus bicinctores*, Harney County, Oregon (photo by William Leonard)

"Miss Potts" with a Gopher Snake
(Kittitas County, Washington)
Photo by William P. Leonard

176